Practical Wisdom

In this selection of discourses, a technique to lead a fuller life is explained lucidly. Some discourses are on a chosen topic or subject while others are in the form of a specific question and answer session. All of them have practical significance for meeting today's challenges in the positive spirit of practical spirituality. The selection has been carefully made by the editors, Dr. Linda Spedding and Petra Kues.

Books by the same author

- **BALANCED YOGA: The Twelve Week Programme**— The book is divided into a twelve- week programme, each of the lessons revolves around a guiding thought or principle which is manifested by related exercises or postures including breathing and relaxation techniques, dietary advice, and aids to concentration and meditation.

  ISBN: 978-81-7822-315-5 96 pages, 2008

- **THE TRUTH WILL SET YOU FREE**—Through this book, the essence of truth is revealed to us under the guiding light of Svāmi Pūrṇá's teachings, and the way in which this knowledge can be used in our daily lives is clearly shown.

  ISBN: 978-81-7822-314-8 157 pages, 2008

Practical Wisdom

Svāmi Pūrṇā

New Age Books

Practical Wisdom

ISBN: 978-81-7822-363-6

First Edition: Delhi, 2010

Published by
NEW AGE BOOKS
A-44 Naraina Phase I
New Delhi-110 028 (INDIA)
Email: nab@vsnl.in
Website: www.newagebooksindia.com

Printed in India
at Shri Jainendra Press
A-45 Naraina Phase-I, New Delhi-110 028

"Real faith does not live in words alone.
It lives in actions, the actions of everyday life"

—*Svāmi Pūrṇā*

FOREWORD

Svāmi Pūrṇā is a true living teacher who can explain in a real sense the profound spiritual tradition that has perennial and universal relevance for all of humanity. When we define teachers they usually fall into one of the two categories, that is:

Those teachers who have information, theoretical and book knowledge, who have some achievement in life and recognition in the world through scholarly presence, yet do not practice what they teach; or

Those teachers who have attained great knowledge and wisdom through traditional spiritual training and through the practice and implementation of the teachings in their lives, those who have lived and continue to live according to the principles that they teach.

In this selection of discourses various key concepts for an approach to living – a technique to live - are explored. The discourses are based on their true Vedic and Sanskrit origin. They represent a guide in the individual's search for universal truth, joy and spiritual fulfillment. When Svāmi Pūrṇā gives a discourse he deals with diverse groups, different nationalities, religions and backgrounds and he is faced with many different cultures. Through his guidance he leads them to a clearer and fuller dimension of life that is relevant all over the world.

The explanation of such fundamental issues through the discourses of Svāmi Pūrṇā offers the reader a real opportunity to understand their message.

Some of the selected pieces are discourses on a chosen topic or subject: others are in the form of a specific question and answer session typical of the traditional approach by real teachers of such living knowledge. All of them have ongoing practical significance for all of us as we experience the ups and downs of life and try to live in the spirit of practical spirituality. To assist readers vital terms are listed in the Glossary and are explained more fully throughout the selection.

Some readers may already be aware of the works of Svāmi Pūrṇā and enjoy the endorsement that this selection provides in relation to other works. For others this may be the first taste of such knowledge. For all readers there will be a unique pleasure in participating in the clear understanding found in this edition. Indeed Svāmi Pūrṇā represents universal knowledge that cuts across all barriers making him a true world teacher.

Dr Linda S Spedding
Vice President
Adhyatmik Foundation, Inc
www.adhyatmikfoundation.org

CONTENTS

- 1 -

A TECHNIQUE TO LIVE

When you do not know how to live, when you are not aware of your own consciousness, *Atma*, the highest consciousnesses, then you are in danger of getting entangled in the details of life ... and your direction is lost.

Once dragged into that stream of thought and tossed into the maelstrom of emotions, no one knows where you are going to land. It is such a vicious cycle, taking you away from your Source and the highest consciousness that you become puzzled and confused. You do not know how to withdraw, how to maintain happiness and stability of mind. You have become so sensitive to your environment that you are now a subject of your environment. Any individuality, on the basis of higher growth, is completely absent. You are at the mercy of your surrounding atmosphere and thus have become a part of it.

However, there is a technique where, although you participate in everything, you retain your level of consciousness at the same time. It is your perception that is important. For example, there is no way anyone can escape the varying pleasant or unpleasant circumstances of daily living. Problems are inevitable now and then. To the average person these situations may appear to be serious matters, but, for those who have known the Source, the *Paramatman* – they are nothing. It all depends on the basis of your view. Take the classic example of someone entering a dark room and accidentally touching a rope, mistaking it for a snake. Frightened, you may react by shouting for help or having some other strong reaction. Yet when brought into the light, the 'snake' is recognized for what it is: a rope. Simply a case of mistaken identity... You realize your folly and laugh at yourself.

Now you see the problem. Any form of confused understanding to which you are so much attached, to which you give so much importance, could be just ... nothing. The kind of understanding you have is like an addiction. The mind is so completely controlled by the habit that you want to continue with whatever the mind has accepted previously – until something else arises to influence you. This inertia, this resistance to any new ideas, will try to hold you, keep you back by tying you to the same thoughts, by repeating the same acts, time and again.

Today many people continue to live in the past, thereby causing it to repeat itself constantly. They reminisce, watch repeats of movies and plays, get fed up, and go to a pub or club, where again they repeat the same actions and wonder why they are still bored or unhappy. When the soul, through constant experiences tries to guide them and they do not heed its guidance, then the feeling of depression sets in and up rises the cry: "O God, what have I done to deserve this suffering?"

The law of inertia is a law of physics and should be accepted as such. To overcome its conditioning, a certain amount of effort, *purushartha,* needs to be applied. There is also the possibility of using this law, applying it for constructive purposes.

Life can be used for spiritual growth or misused. The former will bring happiness, the latter engenders suffering. So many opportunities of life present themselves daily. How far can you concentrate on these opportunities and maximize their potential? If something is given to you, it is your job to create and make the best of that. When you are blessed with a beautiful gift, the objective is to use this gift, happily, to further growth. On the other hand, even something ugly or destructive can be turned into a blessing. You may be familiar with the saying that if someone gives you a lemon, you can always make lemonade. Behind the monstrous mask of war can hide the end of tyranny and oppression, the tender bloom of neighborly love. Compassion and mercy can unfold in such troubled times. The severest trials and ordeals often hold the most valuable lessons. Unfortunately, the human being often lacks appreciation when such blessings are bestowed and through ignorance, greed, or other manifestations of the ego, misuses these precious gifts.

It is entirely up to you as the individual how you deal with any gift or any problem; how you react, how you receive, how you create and how you expect. Here lies the difference between an evolved being, often described as a *High Being* and the ordinary human. The High Being may participate in any activity, eating, talking walking ... anything. But never, not for one moment, does he identify himself with that particular action. He knows that ultimately he is not the one who suffers, who is associated. He watches and observes, although you will find no difference whatsoever in his function or performance. To him all is merely play. This is the example to aspire toward.

Even if you cannot achieve this aim, try to grow from your experiences. Things will always happen. Ups and downs occur every day. The problem arises when you identify with your emotions and physical attributes; I am angry ... I am beautiful ...I am greedy ...I am special ... When you, the Self, associate with something which is not true (you are neither anger nor greed), then trouble arises. You make yourself into a very different person and present yourself accordingly. If someone tells you that you are bad, you feel hurt; if someone thinks you are good, you feel happy. You are constantly swimming in happiness or unhappiness, and how many people will make you happy or unhappy? To grow spiritually, to become truly aware, you have to watch your own performance, attitude and behavior. Then, if you find flaws, you must try to correct them.

This beautiful life is given to be used, to be utilized for development and growth. If you do not take advantage of this gift, then it is entirely the fault of the individual, who will have lost the chance of higher growth.

- 2 -

BIRTHDAYS

Every year people celebrate their birthdays, quite unaware of the fact that this is not just a cause for celebration. Thoughts like "I am grown up" or "another year older, another year wiser" are usually a fallacy. You are not grown up. You are approaching death. Each birthday is a reminder that one more year has elapsed of the time allotted to you. This then prompts the question: "What have I done with my time so far?"

Each year you are obliged to file your financial status with the revenue service. If you fail to do so, you become liable for prosecution. Have you ever considered prosecution in the spiritual realm? Do you submit your account each birthday: "My God, my Master, in one year I have done this ... and that?" Of course; you would never think to submit such an account.

Scrutiny and submission of your financial accounts will make you realize your financial growth – or decline. It will indicate where you made mistakes and how to avoid them in the future. Similarly, each birthday signifies the realization of truth, of death and rebirth – as well as your level of understanding.

Only when death is realized can rebirth take place. Death is your liberator. Death frees you from anything that is worn out. Death is the friend who brings you freedom from old concepts and habits. Death helps you clear away the debris of wrongdoing so that new growth can take place. Say to yourself: "Whatever I have done so far, the mistakes I have gone through, I will not repeat them. Whatever wrong I have committed, I will not do so again. I shall make use of all the experiences and suffering I have gone through, learn the lessons of the past and make wiser decisions in the future. During the coming year I will prove that I can make proper use of my time ..."

Life itself is a great learning process and teacher. Realization of truth, realization of death, realization of the mystery of birth and death ... that is the meaning of a BIRTHDAY.

- 3 -

MANTRAS

It is a fact that the majority of people have great difficulty in settling down to anything that is not for their immediate pleasure. The pursuit of yoga involves time, effort and perseverance. Even if a person genuinely aspires to follow this path, such aspirations may be weak and easily deflected.

Early in the Vedic Age (1500-1000BC) it was discovered that sound can produce vibrations which affect the body and the emotions. Most people have experienced how a piece of music can affect us emotionally, the sound of a car horn can arouse and annoy us, and the mechanically monotonous sound of a moving train can lull us to sleep. By the same token, there are certain sound vibrations which, if combined in rhythm with sacred syllables, affect us on a deep, spiritual level. These sacred sound vibrations are called *mantras.*

The word mantra, from the ancient Sanskrit language, is derived from two root words: *man* refers to mind and *tra* implies release or freedom; hence, to free the mind or thought process from daily mundane concerns and assist focus on the more uplifting and spiritual aspects of growth.

A mantra can be chosen from the many existing ones that have proven highly efficacious, such as root mantras, consisting of just one or two syllables (the most frequently used being *'OM'*, the sound of creation). Or there are more lengthy ones which convey a very definite thought or concept – often focused on creation or the creator (*Purna Mantra, Gayatri Mantra* ...etc). It is part of the nature of a human being to use repetitive sounds and words to achieve a certain goal. Many religions use this same principle of chanting mantras. One of the best known and best loved mantras in India is the combination of "Hare Rama, Hare Krishna". An ancient Christian mantra is "*maranatha*" which is Aramaic for "Our Lord Come". The "*Hail Mary*" of Catholicism is used daily and for the Moslem "*Allahu Akbar*" (God is great) has paramount meaning, as has the Hebrew "*Barukh attah Adonai*" (Blessed art Thou, O Lord) ... and so on.

Then, of course, there is the mantra specifically designed for the individual. This mantra is given by the teacher, the master, the guru. It is considered a source of power, charged with the spiritual vibrations of the guru. It represents the living embodiment of that teacher's understanding of Truth. The vibrations of this kind of mantra create the right conditions for the disciple to focus on his ultimate spiritual goal. Chanting any mantra promotes harmony on all levels and it attracts spiritual energy. It can be sung out loud, repeated softly, or even just intoned within the mind.

You may ask how one can obtain a personalized mantra from a qualified teacher. To recognize a qualified teacher/guru you have to look at the manifestation. A true guru is a living example of the highest teachings. He manifests these teachings both in word and deed. A mantra given by such a being will create a special link between the spiritual master and the aspirant. This link is the vehicle to impart the master's wisdom to his disciple.

Mantra practice is a simple way to create a positive influence on your life. It affects body, mind and soul. The practice of mantra can take place in many different ways. It can be repeated at any time, especially if you are under stress or in difficulty. At those times a well chosen mantra can become your anchor;

something to hold onto while life turns into a whirlwind around you. A most effective way to use a mantra is to establish a definite regimen of daily practice, for instance early in the morning after a bath or shower, when the mind has not yet been disturbed by daily stimuli. It is good to do some deep breathing and, when seated in a comfortable position, begin your practice of mantra. You can intone your mantra aloud, or silently in your mind. Some like to use a tool to assist in the repetitions, like some prayer beads or anything else that is meaningful to you. You may experience a sense of relaxation as the mind withdraws from its own chaotic chattering ... but there will almost always be distractions in the beginning, both from the outside and from your own mind. The mind does not like to do as it is told; it jumps around from one thought to another. Thoughts come and go; sometimes emotions that have long been suppressed will surface. Do not struggle with them; simply let them pass on. Only practice and determination can rein in this unruly part of our nature. Continuing the mantra in spite of distractions, disturbing emotions, boredom and impatience will eventually bring the meaning of the mantric message into the depths of your being, even when you are not *consciously* reciting it, and create profound positive changes in your very nature.

NON–ATTACHMENT

Question: "I get confused when thinking about non-attachment. How can one love someone and not have attachment to that person, especially to one's child?"

Svamiji: "The relationship of parent and child should be one of mutual fulfillment, and I do not say that this fulfillment should be denied. But it is possible that you are the best parent you can be, according to your understanding of that role and yet your child will not behave accordingly, thus denying you a sense of fulfillment. Do not allow this to make you unhappy or feel that somehow you have failed as a parent. Being unhappy you will react and this, in turn, will cause situations which are not beneficial, but harmful. If you know that starting this chain of reaction will lead to a more destructive attitude with further negative results, do not allow yourself to succumb to those negative forces.

Although attachment indicates a relationship of intimacy, a feeling of internal connection with the object of your attachment, it produces a kind of ownership and possessiveness. It becomes a source of constant desires. It limits your freedom of action and imprisons your consciousness. The result is self-alienation, frustration and finally sorrow. Love under the yoke of attachment becomes subject to manipulation by the ego which expects a return on its investment. If the ego feels that love and affection are not being returned in kind, it becomes hurt and angry. Eventually it will turn against the object of its attachment.

Many people interpret non-attachment as carelessness: I don't care ... I don't bother ... that is *not* non-attachment. In fact those who have been truly non-attached have been the most caring and loving. Non-attachment gives you complete freedom. Free from the dependence on anyone or anything, love finds full expression without condition or demand. Non-attachment is a way of living and enjoying life by not allowing yourself to submit to the obsessive and possessive forces which make you unhappy."

Question: "Is it not desirable to be attached to someone and to want to be with this person again in another life?"

Svamiji: "It is possible that there may be a particular purpose for incarnating close to another person you have known before. For instance, both of you may need to continue certain work that you did not complete in your previous life. Or one person may be in need of teaching or being taught by the other. That would provide a definite purpose for continuing contact in another life.

But if incarnation takes place just for the sake of mere attachment, then you are bound to meet again and again. That is the normal process when people are attached to each other by love – or by hate. This cycle may often continue within family bonds, although there may be changes in relationship and gender. In this way you continue to love or to hate the same personalities for many lifetimes, never outgrowing your attachment.

To further your own evolvement and growth you need to develop non-attachment. Love and cherish the other person, but free of the confines of attachment."

- 5 -

ONENESS AND DIVERSITY

Question: "It has been said that there is only One Truth. Yet the major religions in this world vary so much, even in basic structure that it is most confusing. For instance, many claim the existence of one God only, whereas others, like Hinduism, seem to have a multitude of deities. Could you please elaborate on this?"

Svamiji: *"Yes*, this is a common misunderstanding. The world has been told that Hinduism has millions of Gods and other religions only one. However, much of the time we do not really understand the meaning of what we hear or think we know. Many people have a distorted view of the religions of others, because they simply do not have the desire to find out, to think deeply and to examine closely with an open mind. It is far easier to stand outside the situation and criticize or condemn, based on whatever bit of information has been heard, from whatever source.

The many deities of Hinduism do not imply "so many gods" literally, but rather the different manifestation of the One God. They serve to illustrate the many aspects of the All Powerful One.

Think of a human being, yourself, for example. Consider how many moods and aspects of your personality you display: Sometimes you are playful ... sometimes serious ... sometimes amused ... sometimes angry. With each change of mood your expression changes, as does your voice, your posture and your behavior. Let us say that photographs were to be taken of you over a 24-hour period, reflecting all the different moods and activities, these pictures would surely look very different. If you seriously consider this process, you will begin to understand how the concept of "many deities" evolved in religious thought. The One God is seen from many points of view and in such diversity of roles and aspects that a person can choose his or her favorite view, just as you might select a favorite photo from a set of proofs."

Question: "Has anyone seen God with his physical eyes ... and why is God referred to as HE mostly? Who is to say that God cannot also be SHE or even IT, or display any mood, form or aspect desired? Is not God the All Powerful One in any religion?"

Svamiji: "Language cannot reach out to include God. You cannot define God by any human language, or by the most elaborate imagination. If you think you can define God, by that very thought you have made yourself superior to God in your own mind. You cannot define God and you cannot confine him with your thoughts. God is not your possession. Rather, everyone is a part of God. You may consider him the All Powerful, Almighty and Ever-present, and most people would agree. Ancient scriptures from every source declare that God is, was, and ever will be and that he dwells in every creature. If this is so, how can any individual presume that God cannot be anything other than what he or she perceives him to be? God can be in any form, any place at any time. It would be wise to remember this when dealing with anyone or anything.

You are carrying God all the time, right there in your heart. Yet you are not aware. Those that are aware of God dwelling in their hearts are called "evolved", "High Beings", "Saints". The great majority of people, however, do not possess this realization. Their view is limited because they have not discovered the understanding of the Great Truth that God lives within every heart and in all of creation.

Based on the fact that God is in me and also in you emerges the principle that *I am God.* This is a very serious and often dangerous statement. People have been killed for uttering these words. They have been crucified; they have been hanged; they have been poisoned; they have been stoned to death ... Thus, if I am God, then the same is true of you. The only problem is that you have not realized this profound truth.

God created every creature. It is that spark of God within which gives life. Those who realize this see the same truth in every living thing. When you begin to recognize God's spirit within you and all else, this realization will help destroy all prejudice and hatred of those you do not know and do not understand. You will begin to lose your arrogant attitude of superiority and begin to see with the eyes of divine love. What wonderful freedom that will be when you come to understand that you are neither superior nor inferior to others of God's creation. The only difference is your level of consciousness and the use and implementation of that which you have learned.

The functions of different creatures necessarily vary, as do their lives and habits. Lion and monkey function quite differently, as they were meant to. Each creature has its own role, including the human being. Yet humans have a very pronounced sense of superiority, acclaiming the right to use or destroy any other creature at whim. Animals live within four functions: They sleep, they eat, they procreate and they fear. Their lives are governed by these four natural instincts. If the human also lives according to these same four instincts alone and does not grow out and beyond this base nature, there does not seem to be much difference between the human and the animal, over which the human claims domain, except for the different body structure.

What does make the human different is his given ability to

discriminate between right and wrong, good and bad. It does not make him superior. The ability to discriminate gives the human being the job to make society more livable and joyful for himself and all other creatures.

All the world's great religions have the same message. Practices differ according to climate, location and culture. But Truth, Essence remains the same. Truth is universal. Water is water, whether you are in Germany, America, Russia or India, yet the name for water varies. Each language has its own name for the same substance, world wide. Similarly, people give different names to God: Rama, Christ, Krisna, Jehovah, Jaweh, Buddha, and Allah – the same spirit, the same principle.

As human beings it is our obligation to use our ability of discrimination to sift right from wrong, good from bad, true from false. Get together in harmony and discuss and contemplate – in tolerance of the other person's view. Remember that no two people think and understand exactly alike. In the ultimate sense you are truly One, but individually your expressions and manifestations vary widely. Learn from each other through the process of discrimination. In this way you will come to know not *who* is right, but *what* is right. Finally you will come to understand that Truth is always One, but its manifestations are as manifold as there are creatures and aspects in all of creation."

- 6 -

OVERCOMING BODY CONSCIOUSNESS

The teachings of ancient scriptures are as applicable today as they were thousands of years ago; actually, they are much more pertinent today. The Bhagavad Gita tells us that Self is always actionless. It is the witness and the observer, ever blissful and content. Yet the human being, of little understanding and filled with ego, thinks that the body is the real agent. The human identifies with the actions of the physical body and its senses. Thus he is unable to behold the Truth about himself and leads a deluded life of utter ignorance. His consciousness remains firmly tied to the body by the chains of his own karma. Again and again he has to take birth to reap the fruit of his own actions. Only with the arrival of the spiritual preceptor or teacher will the awakening of right perception take place. He is the one who will impart the pure knowledge that purifies the human intellect and lead him to the final wisdom.

Once you have become established in body-consciousness all your thoughts and actions are centered on the comfort of the physical body and the gratification of its senses. You become so involved in the pleasures and pains of the body that you are unable to perceive your real nature, the ever blissful Self which transcends all pleasure and pain. You do not realize that even the joy of the physical body depends entirely on the "body beyond", on the Self. It is a great pity that most people do not understand this reality.

Ego, confusion, delusion, doubt, jealousy, mistrust and competition are all attributes of the physical body. If, despite the teacher's continuous instruction and guidance, you are unable to overcome such negative manifestations, it indicates that you are still very much engrossed in body-consciousness. You need to understand that the more you become victim to those instincts, the more you are the slave of your own body-consciousness.

The Self cannot be tricked. You cannot pretend that you are growing in spiritual understanding, if your very manifestation is negative. True growth must become noticeable in all your dealings, daily and consistently. If you check and analyze your whole lifestyle, ask yourself: "How much am I the slave of my senses?" By the application of the light of knowledge and wisdom you should be able to grow out of such limiting instincts.

Try to see yourself in pure, water-like clarity of mind and heart. If you create waves, you will not be able to see your own reflection. Waves of doubt, confusion and ignorance will distort the picture of yourself – and of others.

There is no room for manipulation and pretense. The Self is always aware of what is going on, yet it does not get involved. It is present in all and it witnesses all, far beyond the confusion, hatred, prejudice and similar enemies, which have been holding you hostage for years and years. The very reason for your birth on earth is learning to overcome, to see through the veils and performance of *maya*, the great illusion. If this task is not completed, you will have to reincarnate again, repeatedly going through the same procedure until you recognize who and what you really are. It is the same as learning to drive a car. If you keep making the same mistakes, you will not be able to pass your driving test. Yet if you want to enjoy the freedom of driving, eventually you will have to pass the test.

The very purpose of this life is to grow in spiritual understanding, to be free from the performance of *maya* and from the net of your own karma. There is no room for maintaining a shield of negativity. Such "protection" will merely prevent you from seeing what you really are: The blissful Self, beyond trickery, confusion and doubt.

Only then, when you come to see the Truth and Reality of your Self, then you are free - forever.

- 7 -

PREPARATION

Webster's dictionary defines the term *preparation* as "getting ready beforehand" also as "providing equipment for a trip". In essence, before we can get into any undertaking we have to prepare, we have to get ready. This is a process that starts in infancy and continues through childhood and into adulthood, until the day we die. A child's entire development is preparation for adulthood; a man and a woman who want to share their lives become engaged to prepare for marriage; the athlete or artist prepares for peak performance physically, mentally and psychologically. Before you build a house, you have to make a plan. The examples are endless. The point is that without preparation you cannot understand the meaning or idea behind any occasion or event.

When people enter the spiritual atmosphere, the experience may appear very strange at first. However, if you are interested, then understanding becomes easier and you will enjoy the experience. Then why is it, that some people are interested in finding a more profound meaning in life and in uplifting themselves, whereas others simply do not care, living life just as it comes? If you are not interested, it becomes very difficult to be receptive and if you do not receive properly, you cannot grasp the meaning; you cannot benefit from the knowledge. This principle applies to any subject. Therefore, preparation is absolutely essential.

Everything in the world has meaning and if you really want to learn, you can learn from anyone, anywhere. As long as your mind is open, you can learn. To receive the thought – to attune – you have to make it part of your life; you have to become comfortable with this thought. Once that takes place, every moment will be enjoyable.

It is interesting that nowadays more and more people become intrigued with the spiritual life through the practice of *Hatha Yoga*, the yoga of physical exercise for health maintenance and for the calming, yet energizing effect that is so sought after in the present hectic life-style. In this process, certain subtle energies are being aroused that can lead to a higher awakening. *Now* you are interested, *now* you want to find out, question the purpose of life and find the truth and true happiness. You may even question your concept of God.

God can be explained in many different ways, from many different points of view and varying states of consciousness. Sadly, there are two terms that have been repeatedly abused and defamed in the course of history: "God" and "Religion". In the name of God unspeakable atrocities have been committed in all parts of the world. Cruelty and persecution are still continuing today in the name of religion.

In the English language, the three letters G-O-D can provide a helpful analogy:

G – is the Generator, the Creator, the One who creates you, brings you into being.

O – is the Omniscient, Omnipotent Observer who watches you - one who is present in every heart.

D – is the Destroyer of ego and maya, the big illusion of life - the one who re-creates you.

While this process of creation and re-creation is going on, it is the Observer who watches you all the time. Nothing is hidden from Him. You may pretend that whatever you are thinking or doing is not seen, not noticed but that is just your own thought. You may believe what you like, Truth does not change.

The idea of "my God – your God" or the belief that "what my God taught is the only road to salvation" is nothing but the product of *maya*, illusion. God is God, collectively. There is nothing else. But when the individual soul becomes attached to all kinds of externals, it gets entangled in the cycle of birth and death which does not stop. Once we are caught in this cycle of living and dying, of bodily experience, it continues. This is the direct result of desire. We create desire and we try to fulfill our desires ... then we suffer. We are born and we die ... we are born again and we die again. We lose our memory of who and what we really are. We get involved in things which are momentary and in transition. We are always in transition, on a journey. Life is a journey, which we consider real. But what is real and what is unreal?

Consider the states of sleeping, dreaming and wakefulness. Whichever state we happen to be in feels *real*, denying the reality of the other two. Thus we are involved in what is not real – illusion. Yet once you try to uplift to a higher level of consciousness, to cast away the veil of illusion, the day will come when you become attuned with the Higher Source, the Ultimate, Absolute, also known as Enlightenment or Liberation. Then all will become clear.

It is important to know that we are all trying to find happiness, but how far can we go to achieve this? We may focus on material possessions or position, get caught in various human relationships. At last we discover that we are disappointed, dissatisfied. We are tired of everything and then we say: "There must be a way of finding *that* happiness which is everlasting and permanent", which most of us fail to achieve because we are on the wrong track. We need to be on the right track, with the right equipment. It is *not* impossible to achieve that high state of bliss. It is not a thought, not a theory or philosophy. It is something which is LIVING, a state of high bliss and happiness.

However, it is a life long process to prepare and develop yourself on all levels: physically, mentally, psychologically, psychically and finally, spiritually. The further you proceed on this journey, this path, the more happiness you will experience. You are attuned to the Source and you will know the Truth. No one has the monopoly on Truth, it belongs to all. Truth is final – Truth is God.

In Truth there is no untruth
But in untruth there is Truth
That is why untruth can exist

- 8 -

RIGHT LIVING

There are many stages to right living. However, what usually happens to people as they begin to grow spiritually is that they get involved with a power they never experienced before. This power is intriguing. Suddenly one begins to sense the deeper, spiritual aspects of the Self, yet so many stop at this point, not knowing the final truth, because they are caught by their own ego.

The spiritual way of life is endless. The more you learn and the deeper you go into the Self, the smaller you become, yet all the time you are growing. The more one grows, the more, one by one, selfish thoughts are left behind. As long as one is involved in one's own *karma*, the accumulation of lifetimes of thought, speech and action, one can never be liberated. Yet unless one performs right thought, speech and action now, one cannot be uplifted. In other words, at certain times karma is binding and at other times it can help you to grow. When you see the opportunity to grow you must catch it; conversely when you recognize a karmic obstacle in your path you have to drop it.

This discrimination of what is helpful and what is harmful to your growth is called *viveka,* a kind of super-sense. Once you discover that, you begin to understand the larger meaning of things – of the happenings in your life. The important point is not to forget your ultimate destination. The moment you begin to sense your final goal, you pass through various stages of development without being caught by any of them in midstream.

While it is considered important to have a true spiritual guide, at times one has to be one's own teacher, one's own *guru*. *This is viveka.* Yet how many people realize that they can help themselves to find their own salvation, their own ultimate happiness?

The concept of 'right thought – right speech- right action' has to be combined with right effort. Right effort has to be made at all times. Furthermore, right effort and right sense go hand in hand. You could say that a sense of destination is the right hand and right effort is the left hand. Unless both work together in harmony, the action is not complete. Every action must be right. One must not rush, one must not grow lazy. Right timing is as important as right action. Opportunity does not come in the same way again. Every moment is precious. Anything that can help you to grow will not wait until later.

In the major decisions of life it may happen that certain events surface that call for a decision on the best course of action to take. In such cases, people that are attuned in consciousness are better equipped to choose the right action by their ability to contemplate. People who want to grow in spiritual understanding will always learn from their past actions, whereas those who do not, tend to make the same mistakes again and again.

Act without self-interest; expect nothing from any act that you perform. Non-attachment to the fruit of one's actions is one of the great teachings of the major spiritual text, the Bhagavad Gita. When you perform an action for another, do not expect anything and you will not be disappointed. Of course, the fruit will come, but through expectation you are imposing your own judgment on your action. Non-attachment is not escapism. The lotus grows out of water but is not affected by the water that runs off its leaves. It is often said that a person of ideal conduct lives like a lotus.

Once you are perfect, every action you perform will be perfect. This is how it happens with the higher beings, the saints, the sages. They are symbols of what they believe and each of their actions; each sentence they speak is significant. It flows spontaneously from within. What makes them great is that they are continually mindful. With mindfulness one can overcome all obstacles that stand in the way of higher consciousness.

The road to self perfection is like love. If one is in love, one gives up the whole world for the loved one. If one loves God, one is ready to give up all for this love.

However, there are people who cannot and will not change. They prefer what appears to be the easy way out. They do not choose to grow. Greatness lies in the willingness to change. According to the examples found in many spiritual treatises, some of the great sages and saints began their lives as robbers and thieves. However, when they changed, they changed completely. Right living is the key.

- 9 -

THE LAST RESORT

It is important for the human being to question life, to find out. The need to grow out of present situations without getting stuck is an ongoing process of growth. Often this can take place very quietly, barely noticeably; then suddenly all is new, all is changed. There may be new insights, new understanding, new attitudes, growth has taken place without disturbance.

Yet at other times, there is a constant fight, both without and within. The fight against one's lower self goes on all the time. Eventually, often after much struggle, pain and suffering, growth does take place. Karmic situations will always happen; life can present you suddenly with great fortune or seeming disaster. But if you are prepared for whatever might happen; if you are ready to apply mind and effort to do everything possible to handle the situation calmly and efficiently, you will avoid feeling like a victim. However, if all fails, if you feel overwhelmed by events and situations there is always a last resort: Prayer.

Prayer is a state of opening yourself to higher vibrations, to a power that is not bound by your own human limitations. You do the talking, releasing the pent up energies, opening heart and mind spontaneously, trusting that your plea will be heard and understood. Yet you do not force yourself to pray – you have to be in the right frame of mind, not motivated by religious dictates and dogma. At the same time you have to ward against laziness and excuses.

It is good to engage the mind in something positive, something that appeals to the mind. Dogmatic imposition does not open the gate for further growth. If dogma and unbending discipline take over, the freedom to explore and find out is gone. Discipline is essential, but do not become its fanatical slave. Rather balance discipline with flexibility. When there is interest combined with practice prayer becomes a joyful experience.

There are some militant preachers who insist that prayers need to be recited out loud to be effective. In answer to such beliefs let me quote the mystic poet Kabir: "Why make such a noise, is God deaf?"

Then what can be considered the best kind of prayer? How about giving God the responsibility of taking care of you, saying: "You do what is best for me"?

This attitude will prevent you from figuring and analyzing, from scheming and bartering for what you feel you want or need. Instead you are appealing to someone who is fair. You take refuge; and once you have taken refuge, you do not have to repeat it again and again. You have handed over your difficulties and the responsibility now lies with GOD.

- 10 -

THE PRICE OF HAPPINESS

The human being has devised many and varied approaches to satisfy himself physically, mentally and psychologically. Then, a time comes when all these methods become exposed as charades. You feel empty – a failure. A much greater need is experienced, and that need, the demand for spiritual fulfillment, will always be there. It can be compared to a continuous pain. No matter how one tries to divert the mind, from time to time the pain will be there.

Some people, having tried for a long time to fulfill this need, having looked for answers in books, in churches, in temples and not found them, gave up hope of attaining fulfillment – of receiving the Grace of God. But, at last, they too come to realize that there is no other way. They have to return to the Source, the Ultimate Reality.

By way of example visualize a bird on a big boat in the mighty ocean. The bird gets restless and flies away to find some other boat. He flies far, in all directions, but there just is no other boat and the bird is compelled to return to the One Boat. Thus it is with the human being, in fact with every creature. However far you may try to run from the Source, finally the prodigal must return. Unfortunately you lose a lot of time in this process. Sometimes it may be too late, for when you come back you are exhausted, lost and confused. Rehabilitation has to take place and you have to start once again.

This constant need for spiritual fulfillment will manifest from early childhood. It is not easily achieved. There will be periods when your longing is so strong that you start searching. You may read, listen to sermons, go to lectures, or look for someone who can direct you, but then some aspect of life distracts you again and the moment is lost. You can compare this search to love. If you want someone to love you, *you* have to start loving, radiating love and this love must be unconditional. Unfortunately human love is mostly conditional, based on and judged by the individual's limited standards. Love is something quite different, love is universal, all-encompassing, total, and it is *pure.*

The more you grow in spiritual understanding, the more you will be able to receive and to reflect this love and its resulting happiness. It is something that once attained becomes inexhaustible. Then you will have found the Source and that never runs dry, like a river going to the ocean, on and on. This happiness cannot be bought, it cannot be found – it must be earned, earned by devotion, dedication, faith, service, sacrifice and humility. It will involve your heart and your soul.

Many people ask for methods of spiritual practice, for purification of body, mind and soul. Purification is essential, without purification nothing will work. For years you may have abused your body and mind, have poisoned their chemical processes. If you want to attune to Infinity, Purity Absolute, you must cleanse yourself. The human mind harbors a conglomeration of various forces, such as divinity, illusion, knowledge, each pulling in a different direction. This is the basis of the eternal struggle of good and evil, the perpetual fight between 'angels' and 'devils'. In fact the concepts of these two opposites are factions of the human mind. The sages of yore, in their boundless compassion for the ordinary suffering human being, devised ways and means to elevate and purify the mind, making it a fitting instrument to work out the final emancipation. Mind is the only instrument given to the human being to triumph over *maya,* illusion. Mind has to be purified by replacing lower thoughts with higher thoughts. Negative thoughts will literally poison your mind. Yet mind is also influenced by everything that enters your body, food, drink, the air you breathe, skin embrocations, etc. You must develop a keen sense of awareness of what is healthful and pure and those things that have been contaminated with chemicals, dyes and preservatives. Religious instructions regarding fasts originate in the thought of purification. Without purification you will not be able to absorb and hold the tremendous power of spiritual energy.

There is no doubt that eventually you will achieve total happiness. If you make complete faith and patience your companions on this journey, all the unhappiness, misery, doubt and confusion will vanish like a cloud. It may seem at times that the cloud will never go – not true, *it does.* But lack of confidence produces the obstacle, wavering, struggle, fights and doubt all prevent growth. Every time you doubt, you fall back, and you have to start again. There is neither the time nor the room to become victim of your own doubt and confusion.

The word *guru* means dispeller of darkness. Doubt and confusion certainly are aspects of darkness. In moments of darkness he is the one to lighten the path. The spiritual dialogue between master and disciple is there to dispel confusion. It is essential to dispel the darkness, that the Light can be received.

And *that* which cannot be bought, sold, found or achieved must be *earned.* It involves your heart and your soul. Once heart and soul are involved, you will begin to feel the love and bliss which flow. No matter where you are, who you are or what you are, once you are attuned to the Infinite, you will receive in all situations and circumstances. Attuned to the Source you will feel protected and full of bliss, and no one will be able to take away this happiness which you have earned by love, devotion, dedication and service, by unquestioning faith and trust.

- 11 -

TOURISTS

It has been said many times that from the most banal situations the most profound lessons can be learned. Take the matter of tourists, for instance. Nowadays there are tourists in just about every corner of the globe. Have you ever really observed them; noticed how they relate to their changing surroundings? Prepared for any whim of weather, they look at this, admire that, check out something else, make either a cheerful comment or sigh at a woeful tale then they pass on.

A tourist knows that he is "just looking", just passing through. He does not identify with his surroundings and the prevailing atmosphere. After London, there may be Paris, Rome and a lot of other places to see. Does that mean the tourist becomes a Londoner, a Parisian, or a Roman? Of course not. He knows exactly where he belongs, at all times. Yet he does not get involved in the local politics or civic issues of any place he may visit. While in London, Paris or Rome, the traveler is subject to that particular atmosphere and law; thereafter not. Finally, if he should be fortunate enough to have a good tourist guide, he knows that after all his sightseeing he can return home safely.

Consider yourself a tourist on life's journey. Wherever you are, whatever you do, think or feel, know that none of it lasts forever. People come and go. Political and religious dogma and ideologies change. The biggest, finest and strongest buildings and structures, subject to weather and time, will eventually crumble. Even the earth's surface continues to undergo constant changes. Meanwhile there are vistas to enjoy, rivers to cross and mountains to climb on this journey. But only with the aid of a truly competent guide can you cross the river at the most shallow point, climb the mountain with the best equipment and enjoy the view from the best angle.

He, the true guide, is the real "native" who knows his way around. Having gone the path before you, he is thoroughly familiar with its terrain. He knows all the possible pitfalls of your expedition and can lead you safely around the dangers. He is your rock and shelter when the weather gets too stormy. It is useless to seek refuge in despair at any of life's weather changes. When you feel discouraged, lost and afraid of life's impermanence, it is the guide who will show you what is lasting and in which direction home lies.

The ultimate purpose of any journey is to return, to come home enriched with the learning of experience. The next time you feel tempted to linger in *Maya's* arms, to admire some view or to despair when the path becomes to steep and thorny, remind yourself that on this voyage of life you are only a tourist, you are only passing through.

- 12 -

FORGIVENESS

Svamiji: You ask about forgiveness' what is there to forgive in anyone? The very concept, based on strong Christian teachings, is not really appropriate. If you want to forgive anyone for a perceived wrong, that puts you in a morally superior position; it makes you the judge ... giving remission of a supposed debt.

It is not helpful to feel superior; rather you should feel confident of yourself and make an effort to deal with a given situation. Try to understand that there was a mistake and make the other person aware, thereby also giving the opportunity to correct the mistake. Of course both sides have to evaluate the alleged wrong. However, if the other person does not see the situation in the same way, try to accept things as they are. Rather, endeavor to change them within the framework of your available resources. The important point is that *you* do your best – and hope for a resolution.

There is nothing to forgive. People have different levels of growth and understanding, based on upbringing, religion and cultural values. Considering the widely differing personalities, conflicts are bound to happen. You cannot change anyone. Often it is your own expectation that is the cause of anger toward anyone. This serves no other purpose than to make you miserable and unhappy.

Before you attempt to judge another, examine your own actions and expectations. You have to co-exist and communicate with others, despite different levels of consciousness. Whenever involved in human entanglements, sit quietly, detach and try to sort out the conundrum. By understanding the human complexity you can rise above it.

At times there may be a strong reaction by one of the "combatants". In that case it may be prudent to drop the issue, although in principle a solution is always possible. Attitude alone stands in the way. Communication is always better than reaction. Recognizing the other person's limitations is a form of forgiveness.

Human communication seems to be one of the biggest challenges in the world throughout the ages. It does help if at least one person is aware. However, if the other person feels guilty it is your responsibility not to take advantage of the guilty consciousness. That is the moment of real communication – and real mutual forgiveness. There is no doubt that spiritual practices are the most effective method to deal with human interaction on all levels and in such circumstances through contemplation and review.

- 13 -

CHASING A SHADOW

It is not possible to eliminate problems completely from your life. The very nature of a problem is to assert itself. However, it is definitely possible to reduce and even to resolve a problem, learning to handle and manage it in such a way that it is no longer perceived as a problem.

A problem can be magnified or minimized, depending on your attitude and perception, on the way you look at it. Take the example of children. Today children are much more mature because they are exposed to so much external stimulation and information and children can be like sponges, absorbing everything around them. However, they still have to go through the same stages of the growing process as their parents did.

Try not to look at them as a problem, but rather listen to them and look for the process that is necessary for children to evolve, to bring more sophistication and the finer qualities into their development.

Whatever is created in life, every thing depends on the way you look at it. Do you see a problem or do you see a challenge? If you see a problem, there will be worry and anxiety; yet if you see a challenge in solving a puzzle, it becomes a learning process.

I will always maintain that there is no problem that cannot be solved. In fact there is a solution inherent in every problem. The only difficulty is that you may not like the solution, you may want something else.

The point is that no matter where you go, it is impossible to eliminate problems completely. You may be sitting in a cave with no one around, then your mind will wander and will create a problem. You may be sitting quietly, living on herbs and plants and suddenly your mind will remember all the delicious foods, chocolate cake whatever, and you will have a problem.

The spiritual master and teacher may give you a discipline, like six months in isolation, living in the wilderness, one year no bread, cake and other goodies, it can be anything and it may appear harsh, even seemingly unjust, but again, this depends on your attitude. If the discipline is accepted with love and devotion, it becomes very easy, even a joy, but if it is done only because you do not want to be thrown out of the master's presence, then there is resentment and resistance and it becomes a hardship. You have to understand that it is your decision on how you take it.

Some of you will be familiar with the example of Milarepa, the Tibetan Yogi, who rose above the miseries of his younger life by submitting to the often extreme and seemingly contradictory disciplines given to him by his master Marpa and eventually attaining enlightenment.

As long as you dwell in this body on this earth, there will be problems. You cannot run or hide; you are caught and you have to deal with life. So face your enemy with strength and knowledge. Otherwise it is not possible to live life. Set your own challenge, and try not to take the average little things too seriously. There is no room for getting too serious about the daily troubles – you will only create suffering.

The mind can be tricked and make you unhappy through illusion, fantasies and wrong perception. If your mind takes something for real, it will manifest as such. It is like chasing after a shadow and the shadow is running away from you. Following a shadow increases your problem and results in unhappiness and suffering. But when you leave the shadow, then the shadow will follow you. Don't follow the shadow, follow yourself!

When we talk of problems, we talk of energy and there are countless types of energy. Try to feel, to be aware of the different energies, like the energy of food – take time to enjoy and relish the food so your body and mind will benefit. Consciously experience the energy of interaction with others, talking, listening, etc – try to indulge and bring joy into your contact with others. All this can be created in your mind, and it will manifest physically.

You have the capability to visualize what aspects you want to make part of your life. There are many new technological gadgets around that are supposed to aid in meditation, but it is better to create your own experience. In the final analysis only you can bring about the results. You can visualize a Spiritual Master, a Great Being, which can bring powerful healing images, invoking the energy of love, power and fulfillment. All this is dormant within you and it is in your power to awaken this energy. This is real.

In the ever increasing conflict of human civilizations, of nations, of collective and individual egos, the most effective attitude in overcoming difficulties is to accept others as they are.

- 14 -

COURTING THE OPINIONS OF OTHERS

It is a fact that one of the most common causes of human suffering is the value we place on the opinions of our fellow humans.

Does this sound too simplistic? Examine yourself: Someone tells you that you are wrong, that you made a mistake, that you are 'bad', or worse, that you are 'stupid'. How does this make you feel? How do you react? Do you feel hurt and upset; do you try to defend yourself?

On the other hand, how do you feel if someone praises you, calls you 'wonderful' or 'really smart'? Then you feel happy and pleased - and you let your ego take a bow!

Of course, your general attitude and behavior will reflect on your surroundings, but do mere opinions of others provide the definition of what you really are?

As long as you dwell among people there will be some who will praise you and others who will condemn you – often regarding the very same situation.

People will tell you anything, prompted by their own moods or motives, their own feelings and their own limited understanding. You react because you are not sure of yourself – of who and what you really are. If you know that your motives, words and actions have been positive, why should it upset you if someone else thinks differently?

Courting the favorable opinion of others can make you lose your own integrity and make you very miserable. A useful thought that can help you assess the feedback from others is: "Consider the source!"

There may be times when you are not quite sure which course of action to follow or how to handle a particular situation; yet by careful contemplation you can often arrive at the correct solution. By way of example it is important to take a stand in the face of unfairness and injustice. This will also eliminate further aggression. Most faiths recognize this. Indeed the Prophet Mohammed stated: "If someone has done harm to you, your retaliation should not be greater than the original offence."

Sometimes we are presented with examples by the world's great teachers and Wise Ones on how to cope appropriately with a difficult situation.

An incident in the life of Buddha tells of a jealous priest who tried to vent his feelings of anger and frustration by hurling a barrage of insult at the Buddha. He hoped to goad the popular teacher into an argument, thereby disgracing him in the eyes of his disciples and followers.

When Buddha remained calm and unperturbed throughout the attack, the enraged priest shouted at him to defend himself at least. The Enlightened One however, with disarming simplicity, informed him that he does not accept his "little gift" of slander and abuse... The priest was thus left to digest his own negativities.

It is valuable to observe how a master and enlightened teacher deals with a situation where most people would react most strongly. Very few can resist the ego's temptation to retaliate in the face of insult and abuse. Indeed, in today's world there is a major problem of reaction and action, coupled with an absence of listening, reflecting and contemplating, thereby creating aggression and violence.

One who truly knows himself/herself is completely secure in that knowledge. Such a being has laid aside the crutch of individual ego; is not shaken, hurt or affected in any way by any insult - nor does the blood pressure rise at words of flattery and praise. In the Bhagavad Gita Krishna says: "One who is not perturbed by criticism, not overwhelmed by flattery and praise, is considered an Enlightened Being". Such a person also knows that if aggression is left without fuel, it will soon exhaust itself.

The truly great teachers always practice what they preach. They become the models to emulate. You would do well to heed them and consider their teachings, so that you may gain the knowledge of who and what you really are. At this point of discovery the opinions of others will cease to affect you. In the meantime, study your own performance, attitude and behavior. Follow the examples of those who have lived a life of balance according to respected values and make it your motto to ACT, not to REACT.

Practical Tips:

- Do not react to provocations;
- If you have to act, act wisely - after contemplating appropriate action;
- Know your own inner strength; and
- Do not assess yourself on the criteria of other people's opinions

- 15 -

SPIRITUALITY AND YOU

Every now and then someone asks me where the best location to learn and evolve spiritually can be found?

Well, spiritual growth is not limited to locations. There are countless places and opportunities to evolve spiritually all around you. If your minds and hearts are open, you can learn from everything around you. For the sake of example, consider that many people have the opportunity to go on vacation. Why not combine the vacation with a spiritual retreat in pleasant and beautiful natural surroundings — a combination that is beneficial to all?

You can have a spiritual experience with nature, and then nature becomes your teacher. Consider the countless examples in nature that humans could emulate: The stability of stone and rock, the flexible firmness of trees that bend but do not break in a storm, the unconditional giving of beauty and fragrance of flowers, the sun that shines on all, on the finest and on the poorest, there is no end to the amount of examples. So nature becomes your teacher. Try to be like the earth, absorbing the many lessons and teachings with joy and bliss. Then carry that in your heart and manifest those qualities in your life.

Others will notice what you have become; they will see the change and be attracted. The best way of influencing those who come in contact with you is by the way you behave and manifest. In this way you become teacher as well as student. You manifest positively and radiate accordingly. If, however, you behave like everyone else, then what is the point of following the spiritual path?

Spirituality is a serious business; it is deep and profound. Do not hide your spirituality; it is the key attribute of life, absolutely the most important thing in life. Instead, feel proud and honored. Be grateful that your life is made better and happier. You are not doing something wrong! Do not hide your belief for fear of negative feedback from the ignorant. Some of you develop a kind of insecurity because you pay too much attention to the opinions of others. On the other hand, some people will ask you questions with the express purpose of starting an argument and even try to ridicule you. You have to learn to be sensitive to the seriousness and genuineness of a question. Do not share what is sacred to you with the profane mind.

Whatever others might do, let them get on with it. You follow your own path; do your own spiritual practice. If you are a vegetarian, be proud that you are not part of the killing. You believe in non-violence. You lead a healthy life, believe in truth and non-violence, in fairness, sharing and caring — why would you want to hide yourself?

Yet if someone really wants to know, you can explain. There is much ignorance in people, also curiosity. If you explain, others can learn. You do not belong to a secret society; on the contrary, everything is "open plan". One has to be clear in one's own mind. The trouble is that when you become different from the crowd you may develop a tendency to feel "guilty", that you have something to hide.

It is important to develop your self-confidence, your inner sense of security. Hiding often results in the opposite: Unwanted exposure! If you are able to explain properly, able to discuss clearly, then there is no problem. Of course you have to have confidence in your own self and reflect this confidence. When you are able to present yourself, others will appreciate and respect you if they have any sense of fairness.

It happens that others may get scared, because they feel they have lost "control", and in a way they are right. Suddenly you have become wise and they have "lost" you. In families, one person may move ahead, others are left behind and upset; the same applies in a job situation when someone is smarter, faster, wiser or just more knowledgeable, then others may become afraid of something they are not familiar with. However, that does not mean that you should stop following your own path and your pursuit of happiness. Why should anyone else object? No one has the right to interfere with or to prevent your happiness. Indian thought takes this a step further — in the spiritual sense: Having regard for the goal of "Ultimate Evolvement", the great Indian sage and philosopher Tulsidas states: "Dissociate from those who are preventing your spiritual growth, however close they may seem."

Spirituality is the crown of your life. It is your birthright. It should be the first priority in your life. *Atma* is of the ultimate importance, it is what you are motivated by, your innermost driving source – although you may not always be aware of it. For THAT you can sacrifice all.

Everything in life has relative value. You have priorities and you are governed by that force in life. Others are dear to you because *Atma* is dear to you. When you are ill with a fever, a migraine or other pain, you do not really care about anyone else. At that time the most important aspect is *you*. When you are happy and well you can love everyone; but as soon as something happens to you, nothing is clear to you any longer. That illustrates the importance of Atma. When your Atma comes into question, everything else takes second place, you leave everything behind.

The processes of growth, of developing yourself, the pursuit of happiness and of bliss are like components of a pyramid. With each stage of life your value system changes. Life is a process and priorities change. Life is change and you cannot afford to get stuck. Make it your business to accept change and try to adjust to it in every positive way. That is most important.

- 16 -

QUO VADIS, DISCIPULE?

A man boards a bus and the conductor comes and asks him "Where are you going?" The man answers, "I don't know. That's my problem. I saw the bus and I boarded."

Is your life like this? Do you know what you want in your life? You should know what you want. Once you do find out what you want, life becomes very easy. Not knowing - not having a life goal - is the problem. When you do not know where you are going, you cannot know where you will arrive; it is like groping your way in the dark.

People often feel that everything is ordained, decided beforehand, and that there is no choice and no freedom. You may call it fate, kismet, or destiny . . . and feel that there is nothing you can do. Life happens this way, how can I be held responsible for what is pre-ordained?

You say: "I tried this and that and nothing worked" But things do work; only results come in ways you do not expect. Is that destiny? You want something but life gives something else to you. This is a classical example: you plan things, dream of things, and something else happens. What is that? Is it pre-ordained?

But if it is all pre-ordained, then where is your personal freedom, your personal choice? You have to understand that certain things are already decided for you and the details are left for you to work out. All this is based on the sum total of your previous lifetimes – your karma. Many factors come into this equation.

I will give you an example: Imagine a cart at the top of a hill. You could say that by considering the design of the cart, the weight of the load on the cart, the degree of slope on the hill and other factors it can be predicted – very scientifically – where the cart would go and where it would land. True. That would be the destiny of the cart. But what happens if someone comes along and decides to give the cart a push and sends it off its predicted course? Everything would change. Destiny is not carved in stone.

Your future depends on what you do now. Actually, you are creating your own destiny right now. You create your future now – by your thoughts and emotions, by your desires and actions - and all these factors will determine your future. You have the power of choice to change the direction of the cart. Life presents you with constant daily choices. How mindful can you be to sort out what thought or action is helpful and what thought or action becomes a hindrance to you? What is your goal in life and how do you plan to achieve this?

A word on the related topic of desires. It is said that all desires must be fulfilled eventually. But when you have a lot of desires, they are all lining up in a row and before you get to a new desire, you have to go through the ones that you formed previously. You wonder why things do not come about in the way you wish, yet already your stance has shifted and new desires are crowding in.

You do have a destiny, but you sense that you have no control. You think you have no control, like when you are in a crowd: you can only go forward, not left or right, or backward - only forward. So what can you do? You have no choice; you have to wait! Waiting is something that does not come easily.

When you are presented with your destiny, you have to accept it and within the acceptance you do the best you can, to create the new destiny. There is no point in getting upset or unhappy about what you have been offered in life. Try to do the best you can, within the parameters of your resources or boundaries. If you are unhappy with your destiny or what you have been given in your life, then you increase your unhappiness.

There is no use in dreaming about something you do not have. Rather focus on that which you already have; you can upgrade it, make it better, fuller, more wholesome within its possibilities, within your resources, and your capacity to achieve, acquire and to be.

For instance, imagine that you buy a house. The house has boundaries determined by size, design, surroundings, etc – and by the size of your wallet. But there are many details you can change; you can move this here, replace that. You have the power to make many changes within the given framework. You may have a tree that takes light away from the house but that cannot be cut. You can trim it. That way you are gaining the light and you are even making the tree stronger. You are improving everything within the given structure. This is a very practical example on making life more fulfilling and happy.

Your life is like is a house. You are given the opportunity to improve it, to make it more meaningful and purposeful. Use your creativity and your creative mind. You can make emotional and social modifications, physical modifications and then you decide about your associations – what kind of friends and associations do you want, what kind of family do you want, what kind of people do you want to relate to and interact with? And who do you wish to spend your precious time with?

So life itself is your material: what can you do with it? What can you bring in or take out? By having the right combination, life can become very meaningful, purposeful and joyful. And yes, it is a challenge, a fulfilling challenge; it should not be torture or pain; but a pleasure to manage. By looking at all these aspects, there is no reason why things should not fall into place. Of course, one can make a mess of everything, but when you acquire insight, then you can organize your mind. In your mind it is all sorted out, and it will work out in every area. These are all key techniques to learn.

The mind is of course a sponge; it will absorb everything. You have to be careful not to overload the mind just like you should not overload a computer. You have to be careful you do not overload the mind with unnecessary data or create a 'virus' in it. When the mind is relaxed and happy then everything will flow and you will know exactly where you are going.

Practical Tips:

- Discard unnecessary thoughts;
- Focus mainly on what make you happy; and
- Practice slow and conscious breathing – remember that the breath and the mind are closely related; slow breathing will calm the mind.

- 17 -

DISCIPLINE

The dictionary defines discipline as: *Training to produce a specific character or pattern of behavior, especially training that produces moral or mental improvement.*

Some people think that just sitting around the spiritual master, singing songs and doing meditation will bring about enlightenment... Well, devotional singing and meditation do play a role in attaining peace of mind, but this alone will not help your spiritual advancement. When you become involved in spiritual training, discipline becomes a necessary tool for your development.

At times the master and teacher may give you a certain task or practice in accordance with your talents and inclinations, but what about those things or chores you do not care for? Let's say you do not care to clean the house or to fast for a day or two, what reaction can you expect of yourself? Most likely some form of resentment. However, if *you* decide that *you* want to fast for a day or to remain silent it becomes a very different matter. Any discipline invoked by you is much more effective than if it were enforced.

Discipline of any kind that you undertake is good – it is healthy and will make you stronger. Remind yourself that you are not a slave to the comforting demands of your body or mind and you will begin to enjoy the task you have set for yourself.

Consider the many direct and immediate benefits to most disciplines. Here are a few examples that involve no real hardship:

Fasting: This will clean your system and assist in clearer thought – besides, losing a few calories is not an unwelcome side effect for many.

Silence: If you decide not to speak for a day you can stop the constant chatter and focus on something more meaningful. Talking reduces energy. Contemplate the power of speech. Speech is very forceful. It can be as constructive as it can be highly destructive. Think of what one wrong word can do.

When you have a problem, silence is a good practice to go into the difficulty and contemplate on solving the problem. Make it a day of contemplation and meditation, a day of understanding yourself by invoking your spiritual energy.

Reading: Set aside one day just to read spiritual and uplifting literature and attune to that thought.

Freedom from Arguments: Assign one day to the complete absence of arguments and quarrels. No matter what takes place around you, you will not be drawn into an argument.

Truthfulness: Make it your determination that today I will be thoroughly truthful, especially avoiding the many little embellishments .

Doing Good: Set aside one day to give rein to your generous spirit, such as by donating time, money or services wherever you may perceive the need. It can be taking a neighbor who is housebound out for a drive or to shop, help with the housework or with the homework of a struggling student. The possibilities to do good are endless. Just look around you!

Loving and Kindness: Say to yourself: today I will be kind and loving to everyone. No matter if someone wants to insult me or make me angry, I will smile and be pleasant.

In short, there are countless things in daily life that each one can explore, understand and implement as a discipline or practice.

Look at yourself, feel yourself and begin to understand yourself. You may not realize this now, but this is the best way to learn to get to know yourself.

If you have mental or emotional issues that need "cleaning out", go into the forest, select a big tree* and yell and shout all your frustration and abuse at this tree. No one is harmed that way and you can release much emotional tension.

The important point is to move on in your development, not to get stuck. Stagnation is serious business. You need to keep moving, growing, learning, evolving and developing.

Time is very precious, do not waste it. Rather, make the utmost use of it. You are here to learn and to grow mentally, psychologically and spiritually. Growing pains do occur, but do not dwell on them; ignore them and they will disappear.

* If you feel that you may be 'insulting' the tree, know that the tree has a lot of hidden inner strength and will not come to any harm by your angry barrage. It really can handle your anger.

- 18 -

TEMPORAL AND SPIRITUAL SYSTEMS

As you know, there are many different worlds. The human world is a world of conflict and chaos ruled by competition and comparison. It seems that competition and comparison work here to a certain extent. But make no mistake; in the spiritual world comparison and competition definitely do not work.

Look at the two systems that have become prevalent in the last century —the capitalist system and socialist system. The original idea of Karl Marx was that of fair distribution of wealth that no one becomes a victim, no one is exploited and no one becomes the exploiter. The dilemma lay in deciding who could implement a fair system of distribution of wealth? It was decided that the government, the State would be the best agency. However, those who supported the government created again two systems: one for themselves and a second system for the rest of the population.

If you were an office holder in the party, you were a privileged class of person. The rest of the population simply became 'employees of the state'. They were told what to do; who will be doctor, who will be engineer, who will be technician, who will do business, who will dance, who will be artist. Everything was decided for the average man. Thinking was not appreciated. The individual had no rights, was not allowed to make a decision. All was decided for you; was done for you. Since there was no hope of change, all ambition died. Why bother to make an effort if there is nothing an individual can do about the circumstances of their life. Thinking was useless, thinking got nowhere; and thinking power also died.

It was that kind of passivity that suppressed creativity and ownership. When you say something is mine, then you care, you feel responsible. When the responsibility is someone else's, you do not really care.

It is interesting that somehow Indian ashrams also work on a socialist basis. The big difference is that there is a spiritual concept in everything that you do because you are convinced that you are doing something *positive and nice*. Nothing is imposed upon you. For instance, someone decides to go to an ashram. There he may select his seva, his service, in keeping with his capabilities and means. In an ashram you will find countless opportunities for service. The important aspect is that nothing is imposed on him by someone else. The motivation for seva, or service, will come from the disciple or aspirant himself. There may be a list of different duties available and he can select one. Or he may enquire what is needed and takes on a particular duty.

It is not a bad idea to make a list. However, when you ***ask*** and offer service and then a task is presented to you, or you are asked to purchase an item, you should accept that duty without resistance. When you insist, you have to pay the price. Moreover, when *you* decide to do something, it becomes a different thing, something beautiful. Yet when it is imposed upon you, against your will, many times it becomes a grind. In your inherent willingness you consent to an act of service, based on love. When it is imposed, it becomes a weight.

This is a very good example of self-acceptance. As it flows from your heart, it creates great energy, yet the opposite occurs when pushed to do something. It becomes a punishment. The ashram concept is focused on you selecting a seva that is fulfilling to you. That is your task, your karma yoga. You can see that the work is the same, but since the emotion connected with the task is different, the effect accordingly is very different.

By way of example, in India a servant of the family is supposed to get the milk in the morning. He goes to the village or to the farm to get the milk. He has to get up early, and reluctantly goes to get the milk. All the while he grumbles. "It is so early and I am still tired... but I am the servant so I have to go and get the milk." He complains resentfully, but he has to do it, because he is employed to do what the master asked. Eventually he brings the milk - a sad and disgruntled person.

However, there is another man, who explains what pleasure he gets when he gets up at 6 o'clock to get his bucket and goes to the village for the milk, and vegetables and fruit from the market. That was his task. Then he brings them home, washes them and puts them in the fridge where they belong. He experiences pleasure and the joy of being of service.

Look at the two examples: the act of both men is the same, going and bringing the milk, yet resulting in two very different effects. One gets pleasure and joy, the other gets pain and suffering. The act is no different, but attitude and emotion are very different.

They tried the socialist system in India. It did not work. It failed totally. In China somehow it is working, but that is not because people are very enlightened; it is because the Chinese government is showing the 'big stick' – invoking the principle of 'stick and carrot'. That seems to be working. Capitalism works similarly. They threaten you with the stick, where necessary, and they give you the carrot when you perform to their expectations. It is the *Donkey Principle.* Showing the carrot to a donkey, the donkey will work. Without a carrot the donkey will not work. This can be true of humans.

In the capitalist system competition and comparison seem to work. Competition is today's heartbeat. This is not spiritual. It is not in keeping with the principle of nature. Of course comparison has its place in the market place, for instance where you compare prices and values. However, intense competition in schools, in the workplace, in the family and especially in sports is not helpful.

Since competition dominates society, there is constant comparison. We compare — we compare ourselves with our parents, relatives, with our friends, school buddies and just about anyone we come across. These two forces, competition and comparison, people allow to dominate their lives. For a spiritually inspired person competition and comparison do not work.

Trying to out-do another person in service or in gifting is contrary to all spiritual concepts and ethics. In the spiritual world you are mindful. You do what is needed when it is needed. You do not need competition or an outside agency to make you do what you are supposed to do. That is a human quality. The question here is, do you want to remain human all your life, or do you want to evolve yourself into a higher human being, a super human being?

The nature of the human being is to evolve. Do you want to remain in the same consciousness all your life? Everything is evolving. Someone once asked me, if everything is evolving, and all of us will become enlightened, why do we need to make an effort? So I said, "Fine, just suppose that I believe that theory - since everything is evolving toward perfection – that I am going to be perfect too, because I am part of everything, why bother to do anything at all, to improve or to evolve?" To this theory I would reply "If I want to have joy and experience, now, and I can get them now, why wait many lifetimes? Why not now? Why eventually?" When you want to have beautiful things, you want to have them immediately — that is also your nature. All of you have experienced that. When you find something you like, something that makes you happy, you want to grab it as soon as possible—now! Not tomorrow. Now! When you want to meet someone you like, one hour seems like one year. You keep looking at your watch. Waiting becomes a torture.

Then why do you want to postpone enlightenment? Someone said to me, "Isn't spirituality better when you get older? Because when you are young, you should enjoy life. You shop, you dance, go to a pub, to a club, and then when you get older you plan on joining a spiritual life?" If you think that *one day* you will practice spirituality, that day will never come. You have to start right now.

You do not realize how much you are missing. You think: if I follow the spiritual life, I will deny all my worldly pleasures... that compares to having delicious food in front of you, but you do not eat. People want to create a feeling of upliftment artificially by using mind-altering drugs. Supposing that you are given the proposal that you can discover something within you that is a thousand times more effective, more powerful than these substances and that you can switch that intoxication on and off at any time – would you not go for that?

Going to an ashram and selecting a true seva springs from an attitude of selflessness, giving joy, pleasure and happiness. On the other hand anything imposed by outside factors, with which you do not agree will create pain, discontent and suffering. Looking back to our two persons who commit the same act with a different mindset and different emotion, try to discover that mindset, that emotion, that on and off switch that triggers the wonderful energy and joy. Positive mindfulness and right attitude can become a way of life and bring out the spirituality in you.

- 19 -

THE POWER OF THINKING

It is unfortunate that so many people create their thoughts, images, ideas, concepts and beliefs on the basis of what is seen or heard – and they condition themselves accordingly. Original thought is not often encountered.

A true thinker, however, does not associate with any particular thought. Instead he passes through the thought moving on to the next thought. If one associates with a thought, it colors and conditions the entire outlook.

The tendency to simply agree with another's thought and make it your own does nothing but block your own progress. To say: "I read it somewhere, I heard it some place and therefore I believe" often results in hard, cemented conditioning with a strong unwillingness to grow out of this thought, which was not yours to begin with. This way you copy a thought from a questionable source.

Consider the idea of "God" in the human mind. People rarely question the concept of God. From an early age humans have been taught that "He" is this and that, that "He" does something or another. The concept of God has been used and abused as a bribe, threat or punishment – at times as comfort or reward – all according to the prevailing cultural and religious background and context. In a worst case scenario "God" becomes the ultimate tool to wield power over the ignorant, to incite war and to commit acts of terrorism. Over the course of history there have been numerous examples. In order not to associate with any particular thought consider your thoughts resembling clouds that are passing thoughts just flow.

It is tragic that people are actually often afraid to really think and to evaluate their beliefs due to the wide range of dogmatic indoctrination and threats. There is also mental laziness. It is so much easier to accept the thought of another than to do the work yourself.

Balanced thinking is most important when looking at religious sources. Such exploration and analysis do not mean that you are negating the thought of God. On the contrary: you are proceeding. You are traveling toward a deeper understanding and fulfillment. You are not leaving God behind; you are coming closer as a result of this realization

Generally people interpret according to their own perception, their own understanding, their own conditioning and their own stage of evolution. Yet Life will constantly push you and remind you which way to go and what to do. Unfortunately this is often ignored. There are "sign posts" at every corner! However, to acknowledge these demands you have to think; you have to contemplate the substance and to discriminate what is helpful and what is a hindrance. It is like separating the wheat from the chaff. The grain falls down and the chaff blows away. Instinctively you know what is right and what is unimportant, helpful or harmful. You do not have to stress yourself to contemplate. There is a spontaneous instinct, a feeling of decision-making in life that will point you in the right direction. It may take a while to become familiar with this process, but then you will know exactly what is right and how to proceed. When food is offered on a tray, you make a suitable selection and leave the rest. Contemplation is like that!

Every day Life itself is your teacher. Life is a gift, but you must realize this. It helps to be aware and to understand the law of karmic consequences. You need to attune to the beauty of Life. On a lovely day, if you are feeling unhappy, the beauty of the day does not make you feel happy. It cannot penetrate your cloud of gloom. Unless you are attuned you cannot benefit from Life and its beauty. Anything in Life that promotes happiness, joy, growth and contentment... practice and learn to take advantage of that.

On the other hand, consider the idea of "sin" for instance. This is a concept created by the guilty mind. It is also limited and subjective. For some ignorance is sin, living in darkness, hurting a fellow creature, not realizing that the sun is shining, is sin, not making life more meaningful and beautiful is sin.

Institutions are designed to stop you thinking individually. This applies to governments as well as to organized religions. Individual original thinking could "rock the boat" of the institution and make trouble. Decisions are being made for you all the time, whereas perennial knowledge is designed to emancipate you. Essentially the responsibility lies with you. Discrimination, *viveka,* is your tool of knowledge. You make your own decisions based on solid knowledge, not on hearsay.

Nature is perfect and complete. Humans can be the disturbing factor due to emotional disturbance. You need to develop your own understanding of issues.

Remember that external happiness is only a spark of the real, internal happiness. If you can discover and tune into that happiness and joy – the Source – you will never be unhappy. Spontaneous awareness gives direction for your life. You have the freedom to choose what is right for you. That is called Wisdom. Force may benefit discipline, but never fulfillment.

- 20 -

THE SPIRITUAL INFORMATION SUPER HIGHWAY

The Akashik Records

Almost everyone is familiar with the World Wide Web, the internet, also called the Information Super Highway. Whatever subject you want to explore or know about, a few clicks on the computer will make the information available. It contains a vastness of information that cannot even be assessed accurately and it is available to anyone who knows how to tune into this technology.

But did you know that there is also a 'spiritual internet? You could call it a *Cosmos Wide Web*. It is actually known as the *Akashik Records* – the term akashik referring to space and ether. Vast and infinite knowledge is said to be stored within the space of the cosmos, endless knowledge contained within the ether. You could also compare it to a cosmic library of all events and thoughts from every creature which is constantly being updated or, if you like, a cosmic computer.

Try to imagine the countless transmissions in space from radio, satellites, both technical as well as human - all thoughts and emotions – the atmosphere is filled with activity.

If you are a yogi, a High Being or highly evolved personality, you can attune yourself to these records; you can tune into a particular area of knowledge. If your psychic wave length is sharp and full of magnetic charge, then you will also start receiving.

Well, you could say that your guru is the big satellite and you can send your personal beam to that satellite. When you have close association with your spiritual teacher it is easy to tune into that wave length and also to receive. But your own magnetic field has to be strong in order to start attracting the positivity. That is why it is so important for your spiritual growth that you tune to a *genuine* spiritual personality and not to get caught by something negative or evil.

It can happen that during meditation something goes wrong and suddenly you are connected to something else – something negative – some evil force or entity. If that happens you may feel strong and powerful but quite possibly also very disgusted. Please understand, both channels are open. Risk is everywhere. Simply compare this to some nasty, negative cyber spam and press the delete button or send it to your junk mail. Make your goal clear and do not get caught along the road by something temporarily tempting that is leading you away from our goal.

Evil can be transmitted in many forms, in a man or woman – it can be anywhere. Most often evil energy is transmitted through a human being. Someone is possessed to inflict pain or to destroy. That person may appear pleasant and nice to begin with but then becomes destructive and evil; although, to be fair, it can also happen in reverse.

The point is do not allow evil to come into play; do not be tempted to invoke this energy; if you do, it will come. Beware of what you invoke and what you ask for.

I will try to give you an example. Consider a light, any light: What do you see around the light? Immediately around the circle of light there is darkness. Light and darkness are always side by side.

If you have purity of mind and soul and strength of purpose you will attract the light accordingly – and yes, you will have tests and trials. Obstacles will always be there, but again, if you are attuned to the higher spiritual entity you can get a boost of energy and confidence from your 'spiritual satellite' to help you over the hurdle. Sometimes it seems that the struggle will never end. Not true – it does; and at times, maybe when you are ready to give up, help comes! Remember that.

FEAR

The dictionary defines fear as: *A distressing emotion aroused by impending danger, evil, pain, etc., whether the threat is real or imagined. It is the condition or feeling of being afraid.*

There is no question that each individual has to deal with all kinds of issues and problems that present themselves in daily life and, if your mind is clear, there is generally no problem. But if your mind is deluded or confused or corrupt, then you have a lot of problems and the biggest problem is fear – fear of inadequacy in dealing with the problem, fear of making a mistake, fear of consequences, fear of upsetting the status quo, and most prominently the fear of running out of money - the list goes on.

Most of the decision makers in the world are not clear in mind; they are confused, often tainted by their own interests and by greed. They may tell you that they have your interests at heart, but do not be fooled; they are not working for you. They work for themselves, for their interests and for their benefit. Politicians throughout the world (with very few exceptions) are working solely for themselves – they may take up the issues which you like to hear, and then manipulate them for their own goals.

Only people who have sincere spiritual goals and who are on the spiritual path can have an objective view of themselves and of the world. To have a clear understanding of what is going on in the world today, that is what is needed. Our planet today is going through many trials and much turbulence, and there is more to come. The element of fear is a pervasive factor. Yet the same process will also bring an emergence of the good news. That kind of duality of negative and positive trends brings also a manifestation of higher energy. One can say that the present time is one of the most critical times for humanity.

As I said, there are countless examples that illustrate fear, sometimes fear of fear itself - and fear can breed corruption. Mahatma Gandhi's life had been such that he had become a threat to the British Empire. Yet his non-violent striving for an independent India had earned him the nomination for the Nobel Peace Prize. However, the Nobel committee, under pressure from the British government, backed off and chose a different recipient. This is just one example of how a powerful committee became corrupted, for fear of upsetting a powerful government.

Fear of consequences, of retribution or any kind of potential threat has always existed. It has never been any different; when troubles strike, people withdraw out of fear; they simply do not want to know. Take the example of Jesus Christ:

Jesus was in the same situation with his disciples – when the soldiers arrived to arrest Jesus, those, not on same level of consciousness and full of fear of getting into trouble themselves, were not able to stand by him - not a single one of the disciples was prepared to stand up for him. When you follow your Master, His lot becomes yours too. As steadfast disciples all twelve of them should have said: "Alright, you take our Master, take us too" Of course, later on they were filled with guilt and overcome by their betrayal. Prompted by their own guilt they tried to make up for their shortcomings by spreading His teachings, which later became known as christianity.

Only when you are on a higher level of consciousness are you not affected by fear. The worldly concerns do not scare you. When you know the truth, there is no fear. Yet fear is the most destructive and binding element in the world. From the day you are born your life is governed by fear. You step out of the house and fear is with you: fear of the unknown, fear of disease, of old age, of death, fear of losing a loved one ... there is endless fear. Every minute fear is following you. Only one who is enlightened has complete freedom of fear. This is the real freedom, when you have no fear of any kind.

On one hand you can say: So what? Let it all come, let it all happen but that knowledge is not easily come by. The spiritual path is there to help you. The more fearful and dependent you are, the more miserable you become and vice versa. The less fearful you are, the happier you are. Spiritual knowledge alone eliminates fear. Fear is part of the human condition; but how do you perceive yourself and your role in life? Do you become the victim of fear or do you have the courage to stand up for yourself with self reliance and see each situation through, knowing it has to be done?

There comes a moment of realization in everyone's lifetime when you are faced with the Truth; whether you can live with this Truth is another matter.

The Truth is your Birthright
No one can take it from you.

ASPECTS OF LOVE

Many times people feel discouraged from sincerely following the spiritual path, because of perceived and actual difficulties they might encounter in today's rather difficult world. And it is true - the more spiritual you become the more subtle and complex difficulties and hardships you may experience in these circumstances.

There is a traditional approach that originates from India in which spiritual knowledge and development can be simplified and very much enjoyed – it is called *bhakti* – love. The Sanskrit term *bhakti* means love and devotion; it is also the path of devotion itself; and it is very rare indeed. In this connection, therefore, I am not talking about the normal human love that is so often easily embraced – and discarded - in daily life. Instead I am referring to a purified love; a pure love that is without condition and without conditioning. This love does not ask or demand, does not expect or judge. Normal human love is not like that. You love someone because that implies a condition. That is qualified and conditional love.

Bhakti can be demonstrated in many traditional examples. For instance, the 15th century mystic poet *Mirabai* presents an example of unconditional love for Krishna and that unqualified, unselfish love, coupled with intensity of mind led to her eventual enlightenment.

In life essentially every creature is looking for comfort and finding it in a variety of situations and conditions. I have often spoken on the different styles of love throughout the world and considered how the term love has evolved. I will give some of the key aspects here. Generally, the human concept of love is more like an instinct to care, to act and react instinctively. It can also have practical limitations. For example, there is a statement you can hear over and over: "I *still* love you", a statement which implies doubt and limitation of time. It says that I am not sure of tomorrow but today I still love you. Well, in some way this is very honest if you are not sure of yourself. On the other hand you are creating a lot of doubt in your mind – and in the mind of the other person.

When someone says: 'I love you', there is one thought and definition in the mind of the speaker whereas the one who hears it may have a very different concept and understanding of love. No one understands exactly alike – barring, of course, the occasional exception. Moreover, later on, when the fever of the initial love and new relationship has abated, things are very different. "If you really loved me you would do this and that" You define love in your own mind. You are telling your partner, that he/she does not love you because it does not meet with your expectations - although at one point you have confirmed that you love each other.

Evidently, therefore, an explanation of love is a very complex issue since you are dealing with human emotions. You cannot see the thoughts and emotions of the real person when someone tells you 'I love you' – it may not be true. After all, people very often act and perform rather than showing their true selves; that is something learned from childhood. Moreover, the concept of love can be too complex, too undefined. You can just about feel that there is *something* out there, out of reach of the human being. It is like a play of hide-and-seek which you can sense. It is a combination of pain and pleasure. It appears to be just within your reach but as you try to grasp it - it slips away.

Of course when you are young, hormones are very powerful and you can get carried away. When you are older, more mature, experienced and hopefully wiser, you are not in such a hurry and you have the patience to wait. Indeed, however, patience has become an unusual quality for many nowadays. You may recall that Hermann Hesse, in his book *Siddhartha,* describes how a prospective employer asks the young monk what qualifications he has and he replies: "I can wait, I can fast, I can think." Now where would that kind of answer get you today? At the very least you would be regarded as somewhat peculiar, possibly you might be asked to leave. You have to have your CV, a list of management skills involving patience, skills of interaction, understanding and enthusiasm for working. In modern times the qualities and human emotions are also of importance – and the demands of life are great. Similarly human love often has excessive demands.

Therefore it is useful to consider the traditional texts explaining the path of *bhakti.* This can assist in understanding vital aspects of love. *Mirabai* , for instance, sings songs of love that she has for Krishna; she does not want worldly love. It is a process of going through the various stages of yourself. It is like meditation, you become one with the object of your meditation. The thinker becomes thought itself. Everyone, at some stage, has felt the intensity of oneness in the process of love, but that is not a permanent state. It is a process of understanding yourself stage by stage. Vedanta says: Be an observer, for only then can you be objective. If you are involved you cannot see yourself, you lack the clarity of the clear crystal waters.

Only when mind and emotions are purified will you no longer have any confusion, your mind will no be longer muddied. You have to let the mud settle. That is why purification of mind and emotion through *bhakti* is important. The teachings show that if you truly want to see your *Beloved* you have to remove the veil you created – a veil of many layers – to reach the purified loves. All of you have experienced qualified love. Now, try to love someone without any expectation. Can you do that? That would be very interesting, no demands, no complaints, but with the simple love of a child. Try that with each other and see how it works.

You ask how you can receive knowledge and love. It is quite simple; you have to clean your vessel. You cannot receive anything if you come with your vessel already filled with ego, pride, frustration, demand, expectation, desire, conditioning, etc. In that kind of vessel there is no space for the true knowledge and love. You have to empty your vessel and make room for divine love and truth. In the Ayurvedic system the body is the temple of God; if you do not make it a temple of God it will be a temple of disease. Happiness, health, and spiritual growth are closely related and they reflect on each other. When you practice a more selfless approach you will benefit from the manifold aspects of love and achieve a more fulfilled and balanced life.

- 23 -

BALANCED LIVING

This is a time of transition with a tremendous amount of changes, both external and internal.

The stable mind will be able to observe, the confused mind will become more confused and get caught in the general disorder. Each individual will experience the changes according to individual manifestation and understanding. Millions of thoughts and emotions are interacting. One has to sort out this conundrum and become clear minded among the entire turmoil of thought and emotion.

Sometimes it is difficult to stop thinking; thinking is a process of the mind and thinking will continue as long as the mind is in the body. So the question arises: what do you think? Do you think negatively or positively, do you focus on illness or on health, on knowledge or on ignorance? The mind is the most powerful source of the body and truly capable of many miracles. It cannot stop thinking. That is its duty. Additionally, the eyes, ears, tongue, etc will continue to do their duties and give constant input to the mind.

Have you considered what *your* duty is? If you are not body, not senses, not mind, intellect, ego or emotion- then what are you? Only when you do realize who and what you are can you truly do your duty. Are you prepared to find out, to go on that search, to go through that process?

In that process there are millions of events taking place. It is like a continuity of elements of mind and of soul. Each event in your life has meaning and purpose. Without purpose your life is literally meaningless. For things to move into the right direction is only a matter of time.

The question is how much do you learn from each event, from each situation, and how much do you understand? How do you structure your life? How do you incorporate the lessons you have learned? In order to lead a wholesome and meaningful life it is necessary to focus on three major aspects: body, mind and spirit/soul.

Do you try to maintain physical health by being mindful of selecting natural, life giving food, right exercise and right balance of work and relaxation?

What is your mental outlook? In the space of one day or in one week where is your mental focus? Do you occupy your mind with thoughts of the daily news, the daily juicy scandals, and the ever increasing violence? Or are you content and cheerful going about your daily routine with a positive outlook and mindset? Are you helpful toward others?

When you are healthy in body and positive in mind, it is a natural progression to focus on spiritual goals: contemplation about the purpose of life; reading and contemplating spiritual scriptures, maybe employing – and enjoying - certain spiritual practices, like yogic exercises, fasting, maintaining silence, truthfulness and many others I have mentioned before. If it is your aim to sublimate your life, to constantly improve its essence, this is a highly appropriate system to integrate into your daily activities.

Remember that all events have meaning. Each creature has a purpose. Lower beings, like animals, are motivated by instinct, inertia and need and ruled by four aspects, namely food, sleep, fear and procreation. Humans are considered more highly evolved beings than animals; humans have been endowed with thinking power, and here lies the duty to uplift and evolve themselves onto a higher level of consciousness. If the human does not use its thinking power or calls another "animalistic", this is really an insult to animals. Animals lead very orderly and decent lives; they have finely tuned instincts – instincts humans cannot compare with - and they live within their given parameters.

Can you learn from animals? Of course! Free from negative emotions, animals do not have corrupted minds. Animals are uncritically accepting, loyal at all times and under all circumstances. There is no falseness, no pretense; their attitude within the limitation of each species is simple, unconditional, and uncomplicated. At times the behavior of an animal can touch you on a level you have been trying to ignore; it can touch your soul.

It can also become an example for humans to emulate. Consider, for instance, the devotion and dedication of a dog, the self-sufficiency of a cat, the utter fearlessness of a lion, the docile and selfless giving of the domestic cow, and not least of all the utter persistence of the energetic little squirrel and the busy perfectionism of the tiny ant. Do you have these qualities? Humans would do well to take a look at and learn from the lessons animals provide.

- 24 -

THE POWER OF THE MIND

It is a fact that the mind is always active in some form or another. The mind is always wandering the senses cannot be still. Mind is like the wind, it travels faster than light. The two Sanskrit terms *sankalpa* – the forming of an idea, making a mental plan - and *vikalpa* - the manifestation of that plan, putting it into action - are like waves of an ocean merging. Thoughts, ideas, desires and wishes are constantly being created.

Patanjali, founder of yoga, classifies human life into two categories: *bhairang* and *antarang* - the outer and the inner manifestations of the whole body, mind and intellect, emotions and ego. These interact constantly on the outer and inner planes. Whatever we can see and feel, everything interacts. Creative politics and mind politics go on.

If you examine each system, each arrangement in creation, you will find it complete. Take the mosquito, for instance; it can fly with the most delicate wings, it has a fine tube proboscis with which to feed, yet it is born out of garbage. You may not like the thought of the pesky bloodsucking mosquito, but if you examine without prejudice, it is a sophisticated system of creation. Each time you examine any system – human or any other – you will find completeness; there is no lack of anything, except maybe your own lack of understanding, your own basic lack of knowledge and of information.

Scientists and others with curious minds have been trying to find out the secret of life in this universe, yet they cannot discover the fundamental secrets although some minor progress can be made on the strictly physical plane. But *all* the secrets can never be discovered on the human plane of consciousness. For that you have to go beyond physics, beyond matter and beyond mind. There the mind can no longer exist.

Mind is a creation of Maya, illusion, yet illusion can be very pleasant, real and fulfilling. Consider the pleasure of good food; the beauty in nature, the delight of good company; no one can escape from that illusion. You live with it on a daily basis.

But how can you go beyond that illusion? In the Bhagavad Gita Arjuna asked Krishna that question and Krishna answered: "I know the truth and you don't. I am aware and you are not aware." He tried to explain this to Arjuna very simply. Well, on one hand it is simple and yet it is difficult. When we forget who we really are, identifying ourselves with body, mind, emotions, ego and even our intellect then we are caught in that illusion. Ask yourself: who am I really, am I body, senses or what? Am I my mind, my ego, my desires, my emotions? Try to really pinpoint what you are and explore one after the other. It is like peeling an onion, looking to find something – yet nothing seems to be there. However, the process of this kind of exploration itself is very rewarding as you go along. For instance, happiness is not just at the end of the road but right along the road. The idea that one day I will be happy is totally the wrong concept. Decide: I am happy now – I am doing this for me!

Once a 95-year-old lady was asked: "How did you manage to live such a long and disease free life - in this world, under normal circumstances, living a normal life?"

When you consider what "normal" circumstances are, coping with the usual daily trials and tribulations of ordinary existence it is very interesting to discover how she managed this. To live in this life with all the numerous processes that go on in the world – the pain, the anger, the hatred and other very negative and destructive thoughts and actions that take place constantly. Living so long in a polluted town and surviving with a positive mind and a healthy body is remarkable, a truly powerful achievement. When all is well and positive, everyone can be happy, but to survive the normal crises into advanced age, that is out of the ordinary.

The contrast to how a yogi achieves that is obvious; he has a totally different concept and understanding – for him other rules apply. The difference is a person who lives a healthy life despite all the surrounding difficulties. Then you have to ask: 'How did you do that, how did you manage to survive in all this negativity?"

So I asked her, how she maintained herself in such a positive way and she replied: "I always look towards happiness and I never hold anything back in my mind." This was the statement from a simple woman – a person without great knowledge and learning – yet she was able to manifest this message of wisdom through her life, a powerful and useful message.

Then what is the meaning of "not holding anything back in the mind"? She does not react to the usual comments or insults, to bickering and backbiting, whereas the average human will react strongly enough to a simple criticism that can raise blood pressure and pulse. Furthermore, when you react to a comment, you most likely will answer back, and this can continue on and on, feeding and propagating the negativity. If you allow yourself to get caught into that cycle you will never be free; you have to let go of all the negative feedback from others and from the media. Watching repeated reports of terror, murder and mayhem on the television does not make for a positive and cheerful mindset. Rather focus on the beautiful and inspiring qualities and activities which make you happy.

If you are aware, life will teach you all the time; in fact, life is the biggest teacher. The problem is you do not heed the lessons and learn from life, although the teacher is right within you. You have the skill and the power to make the choice of letting go of all the daily irritations and troubles. It is always entirely up to you. There is an eternal song full of all the wisdom and advice you need going on within you all the time – try to tune to and listen to that.

Kabir, the famous poet/mystic of the 15th century, was a fascinating teacher. He had learned to break all the boundaries – he spoke clearly and did not hide the truth. Thousands followed him, claiming they wanted to learn from him. What was he to do with all these people? How could he sort out who was genuine and really wanted to learn and who was just carried away by momentary emotion? He finally told the crowd: "If you really want to follow me I am giving you the fire of the torch, you must first burn your houses". Well, naturally all the followers got scared and they wondered: "Is this a teacher or a torturer?" Of course, Kabir did not incite anyone to commit arson; he was asking his followers to leave their worldly attachments.

Apparently gurus and masters have this in common, trying to light the torch of the disciple. The disciple has to be put into the fire of discipline to become purified, so that he becomes like pure gold and this cannot be done without the fire. The disciple has to go through discipline; the more discipline the more brightness will ensue. Of course the temptations are high… All the riches and comforts of the physical world are around you and you get caught and absorbed into this. Then you forget the real goal and keep running after all the many little and large temptations that present themselves daily. That does not mean you should not enjoy this beautiful world; it is there to be treasured and to be enjoyed – it is there for your benefit. The point is not to become its slave, not to get so lost in the pursuits of temporal happiness that you forget who and what you are. That would be like running after the shadow and missing the real thing. The shadow is illusion, maya. If you run after the shadow, it will run away from you, but if you run from the shadow, the shadow will follow you. That is the game of maya.

By way of example, there are some people at times referred to as "fat cats"; these are the ones immensely rich and mostly envied by others. Why is that? It is not the money that made them so powerful in the material world, but the knowledge whereby they obtained it – it is always the knowledge. Of course knowledge can be used and misused; it is the most powerful quality that is being envied - always. If you have knowledge you have no fear. Only knowledge can free you from illusion and all the fear.

As I have explained – outer and inner forces have to be combined, understood and known. It is that combination that will become a total creative force, something to be reckoned with. We may have so many questions and emotional activities going on, that often we dismiss them and do not see them as a power, a force and energy. We get involved in all the little things around us like a child; you may want to keep him quiet and give him a toy – for a while this may appease him, but only when he is fed up and throws all the toys...then he will need his mother.

When you go beyond all the toys and things which have been given and do not get caught, saying that these are not the things I want - understanding their limitations as comforts and support and that these are not the Ultimate - when you have that understanding, then you will proceed toward that wholeness and that is worth pursuing.

Consider how many things you can get caught in. That old lady of 95 has the message – holding on to negativity is like a cancer. Empty yourself of the negativities, avoid unnecessary exposure to negative events and information and look forward to something nice, beautiful and pleasant, look for happiness.

Some people are prone to the disease of depression. To some degree everyone has to go through depression although it is possible to overcome; many of the great people in the world suffered from depression yet were powerful. Depression is like a killer, yet also a powerful force. In a state of hopelessness all is bleak and dark, without hope, without happiness. But you have a choice. Someone may look at a cloud as something beautiful and mystical whereas the other person is incapable of seeing the beauty and regards the cloud as harbinger of a coming storm.

Try to be flexible; if you attach and fix your mind on people, ideologies or similar and identify with that, you will suffer. Only when you have no attachment, no conditioning, no expectation, no fixed desire, will you enjoy life most. The minute you start expecting, you will become judgmental and miserable. Accept life as it is - do not judge, perceive, or expect-and just enjoy life and let it flow. That will change your perception; then you will be in control and no one can take that happiness away from you.

Clouds are brought in by the Wind
And again driven away by the same Agency
Similarly, Man's Bondage is caused by the Mind
And Liberation too is caused by that alone.

UNDERSTANDING CAUSE AND EFFECT

At times it may appear that nothing is happening – yet at the same time tremendous changes are taking place. Take the Year 2000 for example: People were expecting drastic changes at midnight and nothing happened - or so it appeared.

Despite the appearance that nothing was taking place, many things were manifesting almost imperceptively to begin with; then suddenly things began to move - in the visible sense and unfortunately for the worse – all over the world. Now things are changing in the physical world with a definite outward effect. Consider all that has happened over the last few years - it certainly is no secret – there are most visible changes all over the world. The entire world is caught in uncertainty.

Yet the events that have led to this situation cannot easily be simplified, although some people would like to do so, especially the politicians, who would like to blame all the problems in the world on the "terrorists". Never before – at least in the visible sense - have so many people been disturbed as they have since the 9/11 incident. Take a good look at this event and how easy it is to blame all the resulting problems on a few!

According to Hollywood movie tradition the hero or knight-in-shining-armor is supposed to appear in the hour of darkness to save the world from whatever danger looms on the horizon. It is a pity that so many have been programmed to expect the magical hero to appear. That hero is a figment of imagination. When you have watched too many films this can create a fantasy in your mind. You want to believe what is comforting to you.

When people believe something, right or wrong, there is a danger of "snowballing" – the belief gets bigger and bigger, to the point of it becoming dangerous and destructive. It is like living in a cocoon of illusion where you live your life totally oblivious to the reality of the situation.

The truth is that when something happens to you personally or in the world around you, you try to simplify the situation with an easy, often simplistic explanation without looking back and trying to discover the real cause of the matter, without exploring the *root* cause. No one really wants to look at the root cause; it is not comfortable, and it is not convenient. Yet every situation takes time to develop, many things take time to grow before the manifestation of the actual event. Many aspects and happenings finally mature into the end result. It does not happen overnight!

In the spiritual realm, when you want to solve a problem, you have to go back to the root. Take the example of a pesky weed, just cutting the weed will not remove it, it will return. You have to dig out the root to eliminate the problem completely.

Whatever happens, to you individually or collectively, is based on cause and effect. It is possible to look into any situation and find a solution. Sometimes the solution may be quite simple, but you may not be able to recognize it. You also might not like the solution. In any event, if one really wants to, it does not take long to find the answer – whether this relates to a general or individual problem. As the late President Kennedy said at the time of the Cuba crisis: "It is a man-made conflict, and therefore I do not see why man should not resolve it."

Whatever we do in the world, individually or collectively, we do for our happiness. There are two main characteristics present in every creature: the instinct to be happy and free of pain and the protection of the offspring. Consider even the smallest creature; if pain is inflicted, it will try to escape. The basic instinct of each creature is to find happiness, not to get hurt or to be in pain. If you look into the nature of things you will find these same basic instincts in each creature, whether crocodile, monkey or insect - or human being.

Instinct is a natural part of each living thing; for instance, the basic instinct of a flower is to give fragrance, of a tree to give fruit, and it does so without expectation or complaint. It just gives, which is very different from the attitude of the human being who processes everything through mind, ego and emotion – and occasionally through intellect. The tree does not complain "I am giving you so much fruit and you are not admiring me". Now consider how many times you complain to each other in your human interaction - between partners, colleagues, friends or anyone: "Look what I have done for you and how ungrateful you are"?

That is definitely not instinct but the result of *maya*, illusion. When you give instinctively there is no expectation or demand. And once you have given something, there is no taking back and you are not entitled to "compensation".

Living to the fullest is one thing, just existing or surviving is another. Living to the fullest involves realization of your full potential. I said before that the solution is often very simple for any problem. There is no problem without solution. However, there is also interaction in nature and in the cosmos that is constantly taking place. You are part of the whole and therefore you are affected by what is going on in the world around you.

If you examine, you will find that you are made of the same five elements as every creature: earth, water, space, fire, air. These same elements are present in every creature and on that basis you are influenced all the time. It is essential to examine every aspect from different points of view. Try not to simply dismiss anything without finding out what it is all about. That is the spiritual way.

Of course, Yogis and High Beings, masters and teachers have their own way of handling life and its problems. On different levels things are working in different ways. Those who live with higher spiritual values or are sensitive to the spiritual laws and the laws of nature fully understand the events of the world whereas the rest of the human race does not understand and simply reacts.

Often you see something and jump into action without exploring the details and without considering the consequences. You think that if you go and destroy the opponent you dislike for whatever reason the problem is solved. Nothing is solved, the problem is intensified. It is not as simple as you would like to think. Many live in a dream world of make believe and do not understand the laws of nature. Take the example of many politicians. They definitely do not understand; they also do not want to understand. It is not in their interest! They are focused on one issue, on one agenda, and that is all.

If, on the human level, you attach yourself to either that person or that person's agenda, you will suffer; if *they* suffer because things did not work out as expected, you will also suffer. Then their pain is yours and you cannot let go. This is a classical example of how suffering is created by attachment. On the lower level you attach to unnecessary things and ideas and identify there – and you reap the consequences. You have to learn to detach yourself and be objective to see things clearly in the true light. The human mind is so flexible that it can become like glue – so glued and stuck to some particular aspect it becomes very difficult to remove the mind from that track. That is called fanaticism.

Fanaticism engenders an extreme emotional attitude and mindset. Being emotional can be rather dangerous because when you are ruled by strong emotions you can do and say *anything*, right or wrong. This is especially true in the case of human love or in religion (the concept of God). That is the power of emotion; when ruled by strong emotion, nothing becomes impossible. However, one can transform the emotion. It is good to go through emotion, but take care not to get caught by emotion.

You could compare this process with "window-shopping" – you browse and see some delightful goods on display, but you choose not to buy. You use the intellect to make a selection, or walk away. You know your destination and you are so confident that you cannot be derailed. Times are changing both for better and for worse. So if you have to attach or "glue" your mind to anything, why not choose something that will bring positive rewards? You can "glue" to the higher state of mind, the higher spiritual laws, higher state of consciousness. Why not focus on wisdom and knowledge, on enlightenment?

What is happening in the world today is no accident. **Nothing is accident** and nothing has accidental purpose. Everything has cause and effect; it is all part of the great plan. All has meaning and purpose; unfortunately people are not aware of the purpose and the meaning. When you begin to understand the meaning of all that is happening then all confusion will go and you will see everything in the clear light.

For some time Mars has been closest to Earth in 60,000 years – this has an impact on life on Earth. Remember when the media was focusing on the impact of a sun eclipse lots of things started happening. Human beings are connected with the entire cosmos and the effects are undeniably there. We may not understand the workings of the planets but the influence is there.

What I am trying to explain is that every aspect of life has meaning and one has to look at that. Do not simply dismiss something without examining and trying to understand. Understanding is the key. All aspects are connected and when you realize this, then you can attune with that and enjoy. Try to remember that all is within you: stars, sky, trees, water. Identify with those aspects and you invoke the constructive energy which represents positivity. Then you are happy every minute, and it does not matter where the happiness comes from.

- 26 -

LEARNING TO SHARE

There is a well known Vedic ceremony called *Yagna*, a symbolic ritual which is full of meaning. Participation in a Yagna invokes the energy of elements and invites the presence of High Beings and other divine manifestations. It calls upon their energy and power, at the same time offering something in return. A Yagna has both outer and inner aspects. It is a spiritual experiment of sacrificing and sublimating the offering.

Offering anything is difficult for the human being. And yet, the human being has to learn to give. Humans have learned to receive; now they have to learn to give back. Throughout your lives you have been accustomed to receive and you continue to receive. Giving back is a hard thing to follow. But unless you give, you cannot receive. This is something people seem to have a lot of problems with – people expect to receive – giving back is not in favor.

Yet it is the law that unless you give, you cannot receive. Nature is full of examples: Look at a seed you might plant. You put ONE seed into the ground and it returns your "investment" a-hundred-fold. This is a problem with humans throughout the world, whether it concerns giving their love, affection, health, energy or material goods – money being the hardest to part with. It has been observed that once you get hold of money, sharing becomes very hard. Where money is concerned there is a definite block. It seems that that is something that has been ingrained since childhood; some conditioning that money is something you need to acquire and keep hold of.

Yes, people have to learn to share – on every level. Recently someone admitted to me that he has an overwhelming fear that one day he will run out of money. He feels that he can overcome almost anything, but the fear of poverty haunts him daily – although he has no reason at all to substantiate that fear. No matter how much reassurance he was given, the conditioning was so strong that he could not get past that fear.

Let go! That is renunciation. Letting go is the most difficult aspect of the human life, whether this is thought, emotions, ideas, other people, valuables, possessions, places. Whatever it may be, that is the most difficult. Unless you learn to let go you cannot be liberated. You are caught. There is a technique in India to catch monkeys. A bottle with a narrow neck is filled with peanuts and placed near the trees frequented by monkeys. One monkey, unable to resist the nuts, puts his hand into the bottle, grabs a fistful - and cannot pull the fist with the nuts through the narrow opening. Now he has a choice: let go of the nuts and regain his freedom or keep hold of the nuts and be caught! Well, let it be said that the monkey's greed and inability to let go cost him his freedom.

And that is how it is with the human being. You do not want to let go. You prefer to be caught and trapped, going through eternal pain and suffering but *you won't let go*! As long as you do not let go, you are trapped.

Often I am asked what made me renounce. I try to explain, but few people understand why I then continued the process of the human experience to share life's circumstances and to demonstrate that I empathize with the normal human situation or circumstances.

Given that is striving to possess if you encounter one who lets go of all he has, it does not seem normal. In order to understand, you have to go onto a different level of understanding. Let me give you the example of Siddhartha before he became Buddha. Born into the luxury of palatial life, with no concern about daily needs, a beautiful wife and a lovely baby son, he had all and still he was sad when faced with life's impermanence and the inevitability of old age and eventual death. He was looking for something lasting. What was he to do with all this wealth if finally he had to leave it all? He wanted to find something more permanent, to find the solution of defeating death. His quest was so strong, that nothing could hold him back. He loved his wife and child but since he was unhappy and in pain he did not want to pass this on to his young family. If you are unhappy you cannot make another happy. You can only give if you have something, no matter what it is.

So he left at midnight – no possessions, no food, nothing at all, just walking without direction, without guidance, all alone, setting off on a journey of untold hardship that would take many years - with the determination and strength of a lion. To embark on this kind of journey requires endless courage and strength.

The true teacher and master will bring about the situation for the disciple to develop this strength. He will put you on the spot – he will put you in the "fire" and create the crisis that will make you stronger. Frequently a disciple may complain about having to deal with one particular incident or circumstance, one particular person or the other. The disciple will actually question the guru: "Why do you accept this person around you; why can't you eliminate that person?" But I ask you, if I eliminate that person, how will *you* evolve and improve in strength, tolerance and forbearance? Besides, that person has a role to play; he or she is the tool for your advancement.

It is the technique of the Master to test you in difficult situations. When all is well and as long as no one disturbs you all is fine - you may be the perfect disciple, person or being, but when the storm blows, how strong can you be to withstand the impact? At times you may feel you are being "tortured" by your Master, then how do you act and react, how much patience do you have, how much love do you have, and how much understanding and faith do you have when someone is making your life difficult? The spiritual path is full of pleasure, love, enjoyment and care and yet it is not an easy path for often it is also covered with thorns. The Master's idea is to help the disciple to let go of the old attachments and to bring out the perfection in the disciple. This is equally true of any challenges encountered along the spiritual path.

Another related point is the concept of sharing: A key element of the spiritual path is generosity and kindness. Only when you learn to give, can you receive. Give without being asked to do so – share what you have – do not hoard. Share your food, your goods, your time, your skills, and your money, whatever you have.

The Yagna is an act of offering and receiving: you offer five grains to represent the five symbolic elements. By recognizing these elements and inviting High Beings, the Yagna becomes an invocation of power and energy. You offer your ego, your love, respect and gratitude. By these means you receive; you can prosper, increase your happiness, achieve peace and walk to your destination. Thus, through such offering and the sharing experience your life becomes fulfilling.

THE GURU/DISCIPLE RELATIONSHIP

Many times I have been asked - to the point of interrogation - about the relationship between the Sat-Guru (that is the Ultimate Guru, rather than all the many gurus along the way) and the disciple; what it entails, what it should be, what could be expected, what it "costs", and many more pertinent- as well as impertinent- questions. Only very few of such questioners truly want to understand the dynamics of this sacred relationship; for those I shall try to explain:

In the East the close relationship between Guru and disciple is well recognized and accepted, a tradition going back to Vedic times. Put simply, it is the relationship between God and the individual soul.

Therefore, the search for and the recognition of the Guru, the ultimate teacher, is considered the most important step in the serious seeker's quest for Truth. This kind of seeker will listen to his heart and inner wisdom with objectivity to avoid the challenge of highly developed psychic powers with no corresponding spiritual evolution. He will search until he finds the Master who speaks to his heart and who is able to confer the highest truth and wisdom with no other motive than love for humankind at large. Fortunate indeed is the seeker who finds such a Master.

At this point the traditional seeker from the East more often has the cultural and environmental advantage of his upbringing which taught him profound respect, love and reverence for parents, elders and teachers - qualities which are in sad decline everywhere now, especially in Western culture. Such a student is very much aware of the sacredness of the Guru/disciple relationship.

In comparison, the average Western aspirant, in ignorance often blunders his way into the presence of a teacher of whom he may have heard, without understanding who and what it is the teacher represents. He behaves according to his own background's code of courtesy, no more. He may make a "deal" of give and return on the basis of 'you teach me and I'll give you' He may ask, or beg for, even demand certain instructions or initiations, dictate how, where, when and what he is to be taught and may try to figure out how much time he can "spare" from his other activities. He questions what this teacher can give. Although such thoughts and beliefs may not be voiced out loud, they can run subtly through the uninformed seeker's consciousness.

Conditioned by his own importance and worldly achievements he measures the Guru's knowledge and wisdom by his own limited standards. More than that, he informs the Guru on how learned he, the hopeful candidate, is and what future plans he has decided on.

It also happens that a student, attracted by the high vibration of the Master, may truly feel the closeness between his soul and his teacher. Yet in an attempt to express this closeness he may allow his behavior to degenerate into familiarity, even thoughtless disrespect. Such slap-on-the-shoulder attitude is as inappropriate to the sanctity of the relationship, as well as to the seeker's spiritual development. The result is that he learns nothing. Eventually he returns to his old life, sad and disappointed, sometimes angry, but certainly no wiser and with the thought that this famous teacher knows nothing after all. This conduct is increasingly occurring in the East nowadays.

Please understand that these observations are not intended as a slight on the Western aspirant. They do, however, illustrate the need to adapt, to be open, to learn and to change when entering a previously unknown or unfamiliar situation. In countries which have let the tradition of Guru/disciple relationship lapse, the spiritual teacher has been reduced to a mere lecturer who collects his fee after filling the pupil's head with much and varied information and then both teacher and pupil go their separate ways. Under such circumstances spiritual unfoldment and growth become impossible.

How then is the spiritual seeker to approach the Master or Guru? How should he present himself? How should he behave?

A variety of enlightened writings in literature and poetry expound the necessary qualities to be fit to be called a spiritual seeker; the serious seeker has to pay the whole fee; he has to surrender all. "Only then, in humility, can he begin his service to the Beloved, to his Master and to his God" (from "The Garden of the Beloved").

I have spoken of Milarepa, the great Tibetan Yogi before. When he approached his elected teacher, Marpa, he did not just go with cap in hand, but with infinite respect, bowed low and on his knees in humble obeisance. He offered himself, body, mind and speech, and was prepared to go through any discipline at the hands of the Great Master to obtain the teachings of truth. He entered the Guru's service, ready to do the most menial tasks out of love and devotion and not for fear of the Guru's scorn or punishment – although he got plenty of both. Milarepa knew that he was the one on trial, that he had to prove his worthiness to be taught. The desire for liberation was not enough; he also had to deserve.

On that basis, once the seeker has found his divinely appointed teacher and has been accepted, a unique form of relationship can be developed. This is the only relationship whereby higher learning can be transmitted.

If the new disciple can retain the awareness of who and what his Guru is, there should be no problem. The disciple has to overcome any conditioning and his reluctance to acknowledge the concept of God or divinity in human form. His behavior will naturally change, even if he continues to adhere to many customs of his upbringing. By way of example, although great beauty and profound symbolism can be demonstrated through gestures of homage, genuflection and prostration, it should be remembered that the spirit of obeisance does not lie in the knees, but in the heart.

Respect and love for the Guru or Master is expressed naturally in the disciple's thoughts, speech and actions. He obeys implicitly, without questioning, without criticism and definitely without argument. He bears all comments and disagreeable instructions without complaints and carries them out faithfully. That is why faith and trust must be complete.

As his respect and love for the teacher grow, attunement results and inappropriate behavior will naturally fall away. Striving to attain the above qualities, the disciple continues on his way, led by and cared for by his Guru until liberation is attained. How long this will take and when this will happen generally depends on the disciple alone.

- 28 -

AVOIDING EMOTIONAL DERAILMENT

A man had reached 100 years. This was the headline in the news and the man was being interviewed: "How did you manage to live so long and remain in good health?"

The man replied: "I made sure I did not forget to breathe, and I took frequent holidays." This may sound very simplistic, but essentially the man was trying to explain his lifestyle. He may not have expressed himself very poetically, but when you contemplate what he said, it is actually quite profound. Breathing and relaxation become a lifestyle of physical discipline like exercise and walking, enjoying nature around you. These are all things that promote the breath of life – *pranayama.* As long as you breathe, life is sustained. You need to understand your physical body and your mind.

It is so important to unwind, to release the daily hassles and irritations, all the nagging disturbances in your life. If you examine your days, there are very few incidents, thoughts, aspects, etc that give you pleasure. For instance, at work, you get the message that "the boss wants to see you". What do you expect, what thoughts come into your mind? Is it fair to say that you may anticipate problems, conflict perhaps?

It is understandable that sometimes you want to run away from society – what you have created is not conducive to your health and happiness. Your environment, created by you, is not beneficial to your well-being. This lack of well-being is what you are missing. So sometimes you just want to run away, as far as possible, to get away from all the unpleasantness – hoping that a distant place or land will give you some peace. For some time that may provide a temporary answer, but it is not a permanent solution. Try to find the permanent solution instead - a technique whereby you can enjoy life. The whole idea of following the path of yoga is to unite yourself, to feel one with oneness; to feel that you can connect yourself with the whole completely and that you are able to discipline yourself, to focus your mind and to grasp that essence. The final endeavor and goal should be to integrate all aspects of yourself and to be able to relax even while in the midst of contradiction, controversy and conflict. The mind is so powerful that the lifestyle you have created for yourself is producing so much disturbance that you feel you cannot escape. What is the solution?

There is only one solution. You have to go through it. If you are scared of the darkness, you have to go through it, go through your own fear. For disciples to learn this technique the teacher can create circumstances to throw them into a crisis to see how you manage. If a captain does not have a storm at sea, how can you evaluate the caliber of the captain? The disciple has to prove himself or herself in a storm created by the teacher.

How do we know that all that we learn is right unless we go through it? Life itself is a great challenge to be faced. Imagine that when you wake up every morning you dread the day. Instead try to focus on all the little things of comfort you have done a 1000 times, yet you look forward to. Maybe the day will come when you say "enough" but you continue to look forward. You cannot just give up; for 'enough' will be the end of you. But it can also be the beginning.

By way of example, one young and educated disciple, Narendra, approached his teacher with arrogance and rudeness, his attitude was blunt and condescending. He looked at the great teacher with contempt, thinking "what can he teach me, I know it all". He was filled with adolescent self-importance, and with the energy and conceit of youth. The mind can create a mistaken identity: Narendra made an assessment of the teacher based on his limited experience. Only after years of service did he begin to understand who he was dealing with. Eventually he became known as Svami Vivekananda, one of the most influential spiritual teachers of the philosophies of *Vedanta* and *Yoga.*

When you think you are the body and identify with it, remember that the photo on your passport, for example, is not really *you*. Your external appearance is merely your 'cover', your façade. You measure yourself on physical and emotional levels. Look at the calm sea, there is no wind, then watch it during a storm: what do you see? Wild waves of enormous height. That is also part of you. Basically you may be calm and controlled, you are not possessive, you do not identify with your desire, anger, greed, and your attachment. But at the same time you have accepted your waves of anger and identified with them and when you are angry you feel destructive. All the many manifestations come upon you like ocean waves and when you are caught into the waves you forget who you are – and you are lost.

That is what Sri Ramakrishna tried to explain to the young Narendra, when he questioned him: "How do we know that what you say is right?" At that time, it is said, the teacher threw him into the deep water even though Narendra could not swim. When he felt he was drowning, the teacher rescued him. The young man then accused Sri Ramakrishna: "How can you be a teacher, you were trying to drown me. Then Sri Ramakrishna asked: When you were drowning, what were you thinking?"

"Thinking? How could I think of anything except trying to survive?" the young man replied

That is the kind of intensity that is necessary to progress. Do you have that intensity to learn? When you have that intensity and longing to learn, then the ground is prepared for growth. The seed has always been there but the ground has to be prepared. All the elements have to be in right order. Then creation starts, and you can see the explosion of energy and life.

When there is readiness, take the opportunity that presents itself. You must learn both: to give and to receive. You cannot just receive. Look at the earth, one seed multiplies a thousand fold. You must receive and you must give back; it is the law of nature.

Life has to be in complete balance without extremes – any extreme can destroy you. Buddhists and Aristotelians advocate the Middle Path which spells balance. Love and hate are the two extremes that can cause disaster. Extremism is nothing new and must be avoided. Ideologies often demonstrate that you cannot change anyone by force, throughout time and history and throughout the world. There is no need for extremism ever, yet in continues. Extremists want to change the world, but they can not do so. You cannot change others; crusades of any kind do not work, whether national, international, religious or family crusades. The only thing you can do is: Change yourself!

If I tried to change people by my own expectations I would not be here. People often want to create a fantasy, live in fantasy. You set a target which may be something you perceive as lacking in your life, like a house, children, a spouse, or a holiday. So you create a fantasy around the object of your desires. Basically you are not satisfied with what you have and you want more. That only shows your desperation; you may think that once you had some happiness and you want it all restored. That desperation to regain whatever it is does not help you. The teacher shows you the balanced path but the teaching is often ignored.

People often ask me: "What qualification do I need to be in touch with you?" The answer is simple: Sincerity!!! That word covers everything. Catch hold of this one thing and all else will come. Seize the main root of happiness. It is no good jumping from branch to branch; instead look at the root of happiness and don't get side tracked. Then you will have all the benefits. Emotions are so powerful, but if you get caught, you create confusion. Self sufficiency is important and the spiritual path will help you to become more self reliant.

There are some so-called teachers who try to keep others needy and in ignorance; they would rather keep their knowledge secret, maybe because of some insecurity of being no longer needed after parting with their knowledge. But knowledge is to be shared. The bond between teacher and student becomes much stronger if you share; the relationship becomes deeper and more powerful. The true teacher/disciple relationship is eternal and does not end. Knowledge is perennial, it never runs out and it is never boring. We have to examine ourselves – the idea is to create a wholesome life, leaving all our little attachments, addictions and easy answers.

Maximum benefit is only achieved when you implement the spiritual techniques in your daily life. When you practice daily you will be happy every day. It is like a recharge for you and this battery will never die – you can compare it to a spiritual trickle charge. It will keep you on the right track and your train to happiness will not be derailed. Try to avoid any emotional derailment. It saddens me to see people emotionally derailed. When you are caught into a situation where you do not restore normalcy to your mind, you are in danger of derailment. Remember to get back on track before the wreckage and emotional debris is too much to clear.

- 29 -

EVOLVING INTO WHOLENESS

It is said that everything is evolving all the time in an ongoing, continuous process of growth. Consider the outside world and observe how it is changing and developing constantly, not only in the sense of what you are not aware of, but also how it impacts on your daily lives.

Humans are very much involved with the innovation and the development of all external aspects. Small technical things like cell phones, computers, etc are a recent phenomenon. Today all the technological gadgets have become extremely important throughout the world. Yet humanity lived without such hi-tech gimmicks for centuries. What has now become an integral part of daily life you may feel you cannot do without. You know that evolution is taking place all around you – but can you say that without cell phones, laptops, TV, etc you were less evolved?

What happened before all this advancement of technology? The knowledge, the information has always been there; it simply had not yet been discovered. Consider the discovery of a new world, like the American continent; it had always been there, but it had remained outside the awareness of the European explorers. In the same vein, there also used to be a belief that the earth was flat! The point is that just because you do not know something - you are not aware of it, or have not found out about it yet - does not belie the existence of anything. Once found, once discovered, that knowledge becomes part of you.

This act of discovery is the real key of your life. How can you achieve that? Well, you can start by simply looking around you and observing every day. By such observation you are evolving and this is an ongoing process. Then what happens when finally all has been discovered, when evolved to that final crescendo – then what have you found? What is the end, the final accomplishment? What is supposed to become of us all? Where does it all end? These are vital questions.

Is your consciousness your destiny? That process of an ongoing search continues whether you realize it or not, even in sleep. You may suddenly wake up and discover that some significant event has happened. That's why normal human behavior is to turn on the radio, TV, etc. People generally want to make sure that they have not missed anything that may affect them. However, can you say that a yogi sitting in a cave in the Himalayas who has not listened to the latest news is less knowledgeable or evolved? This involves more food for thought.

There are constant discoveries taking place around us, one of the more recent ones being the creation of electricity from the ocean. This creates a vast and seemingly endless opportunity. Yes, the world can change in many ways, yet often the more important and urgent issues are not being addressed. There is an energy crisis. Global warming – and climate change - represents the biggest challenges for the world. They can upset the entire equilibrium of the planet, disturbing earth's delicate balance. Such problems sometimes appear insoluble.

Vedanta says that every problem can be solved - you are the Ultimate and you have all the power and knowledge – and if you are a completely evolved being, where is the problem? The problem arises when you identify with your human limitations, feeling helpless that you cannot change things. This seems a major contradiction. Yet humans are contradictory in nature. Within the concept of maya, the play of life, you create a game and a puzzle. When maya, the illusion of life, is at work, mind creates illusion and delusion and you can delude yourselves about anything.

Basically you are free to do as you like. This may seem a very complex process for humanity – on one hand you are powerful to create and innovate and on the other hand quite helpless to deal with the fallout of what you have created. This is a puzzling thought; you do not know what you really want – despite much search and longing. You should ask yourself what exactly are you looking for and why are you looking.

Most of you are familiar with the term window-shopping. You walk through the market, looking at all the shops and all the wares on display, but you do not buy. Try to adopt the same detachment to the daily temptations of all worldly displays. You are passing through the world but you are not going to be caught by the trappings of the world which are everywhere. Instead find out who you really are. Traditionally speaking, it is the guru who rescues the disciple from the various trappings.

There is no denying that is easy to get caught in the trappings of the world. It is a process of life, that whatever is created, nothing is to be rejected. There are situations you don't want to see, do not want to face, to understand or consider. So you make a mental taboo. Death is a good example; you do not want to talk about it, or deal with its approach, although it is the inevitable end for all. Instead you talk about and celebrate birthdays; then you say "How old are you? You look so young." It is the idea of compliment everyone likes, like praise. Yet deep down you know exactly what is going on – you are not fooled yourself and yet you love the compliments. This psychological deception brings to mind the illusion of the ostrich that hides his head in the sand, pretending it is safe.

Humans have the same concept of illusion by pretending something will not happen. You do not want to see the reality and so keep things as they are. But you cannot hide from yourself; for wherever you go you carry yourself. That is why you are the best teacher, the best to observe yourself. Others can help but you have to understand your own role: this role is not to be underestimated. Whatever may be happening in the external universe – you also carry the internal universe. The outside is merely a reflection. By way of example you may create a notion, an idea or thought that someone is looking at you, observing you – although this is not so – to the extent that you become imprisoned by the perceived thoughts and looks of others (paranoia). It is always up to you, how you reflect, interact or see the world outside of you. Try this: you wake up in the morning, go out and smile at everyone. In embarrassment they may just smile back. It is YOU who is creating and reflecting on the outside world.

It is like looking at the world through colored glasses. Take sunglasses for example: your mind sees things in a different light although the scenery is the same. What kind of mind-coloration do you want, what kind of perception do you want to ingrain? How do want to regard the world outside you?

It is your own eye which creates the concepts of how you judge the world. It is YOU actually. In the process of evolution many things will happen; you look outside yourself and believe what you want to believe. There is the example of the Kokila or Koel bird holding up the sky; it lies on its back, both feet held high and believes that it has the job to stop the sky from falling.

You alone have the power to change your perception to evolve yourself in order to become whole or complete. See clearly what is what, for by looking and examining and analyzing everything, you become clear-sighted with clear understanding of all things belonging to this world and you will know that you, yourself, are part of it. That is why one of the most prominent Vedic scriptures, the Yayurveda, states:

Om Purnamadah Purnamidam Purnat Purnamudachyate, Purnasya, Purnamadaya, Purnamevavashisyate

"That is Whole, this is Whole, Whole comes out of Whole.
If Whole is subtracted from Whole, still Whole is left."

*Yajurveda**

* Purna (Whole) is derived from the root "Pri" meaning to fill. Thus Purna means full or complete. In this verse, Purna can also be interpreted to mean infinity, totality and completeness. The second line then yields that the result of subtracting infinity from infinity is still infinity.

- 30 -

HEALTH MANAGEMENT SYSTEM

I have explained many times that good health is a first condition to advancing yourself in any way. Modern living, however, does not make this very easy. Media advertising especially bombards you daily with countless items, products and gadgets on the market that are supposed to make you "healthy, wealthy and wise", implying that without any of these you cannot have a healthy and happy life.

Do you accept all these statements? Or do you try to analyze and inform yourself? You live in the body that you are born with and for all intents and purposes you are responsible for its maintenance. You could compare this with a mechanic looking after an engine that, in order to function at peak performance has to have the correct fuel and lubrication It has to be cleaned regularly, maybe adjusted, and then it is made to run and function.

Similarly, your body's fuel needs to consist of fresh, unprocessed and balanced food. Food which has been processed only pollutes your system, introducing sickness to your body by countless additives and chemicals. It also does not have the same energy as fresh food. Regular effective elimination is equally important, as is the need to make your body move, in other words, exercise. One is reminded of the little saying: ***If you rest, you rust.***

Based on all of the above information you need to establish your own health management system. You have the knowledge, the power and the ability to establish this yourself. People are selling information all the time, often obscuring, even avoiding, the truth. In the commercial world health has become a business and the only thing that really matters is the "bottom line" - the money the business generates.

Yet things have changed with the cyber age and information is readily available to anyone. This may be good in one way, but can be dangerous in another way when a *little* knowledge can confuse the issue further if you do not make the effort to understand the whole picture.

A true health management system is based on knowledge. First you need to inform yourself of some basic functions of your body – and this information is easily obtained by mindfully reading or studying, then analyzing, what you have read. Then you can take charge of yourself, instead of relying on your doctor. By all means get information and advice from your physician. Discuss with him/her what is in the best interest of your health. That way you become partners in your health management. But essentially it is you who has to make the decision of what is right for you. You become pro-active and that is real health management, not just depending on your doctor to fix any health problems.

Any responsible health care practitioner will encourage you to be conscientious in taking care of yourself. You alone have the power to become healthy – everyone and everything else can be a contributing partner in your health. It is even more important to focus on preventive health rather than having to repair those problems that have already manifested. Get a regular checkup of your body by your physician and by your dentist *before* things go wrong, before pain and decay manifest and before symptoms become overwhelming. Only then will you have the choice to make the decisions that will allow your body to perform efficiently and for a long time. Only then will you have the energy and strength to take you further toward your spiritual goals.

SOME THOUGHTS ON MEDITATION

Many times I am asked about the most favorable conditions for meditation. Certainly your surroundings do matter. For instance, being out in the beautiful countryside is helpful in relaxing your mind; and relaxation is vital for inducing a state of meditation. If at all possible, try to seek a place for meditation in a quiet or calm setting such as in the forest where there are few, if any, disturbing sounds. This is especially helpful after a rain which clears the atmosphere of pollution. Of course, if in the city, any tranquil space will do.

Consider, for example, the difference in listening to the sounds of nature - a gentle breeze that rustles the leaves in the trees, bird song, a babbling brook - against being in the middle of a hectic road in a city with all its disturbing noise and pollution. The variation of sound is endless – and the mind responds to all. Mind is always subject to its surroundings yet mind needs quietness for entering a meditative state. It is the nature of mind to move from one thing to another; for this reason meditation should not be attempted while the mind is agitated.

Try this exercise to calm the mind. Settle yourself comfortably and just observe your breath, let your breathing become deeper and more regular and you will find the mind responding to your calmed and slowed breath. Remember also that mind and breath are very closely related, the slower the breath, the calmer the mind.

Conversely, when you are excited your breathing will be shallow and rapid. As a matter of interest, you could try to observe how your breath rate changes during your daily activities.

The aim of meditation is to merge with the object of your meditation. Meditation is a gradual process. You begin with concentration, followed by contemplation and finally you enter the state of meditation, of oneness. In the true state of meditation you, the meditator and the mind become one; you lose all sense of time and place. It is similar to a state when you are very tired, such as after a long journey. You may have dozed off, then you awaken, maybe a little perplexed, and for a few seconds you wonder where you are. For a moment you have lost the sense of time and space.

Now, this should not just happen when you are tired and/or after a long sleep. That condition should come automatically when in a state of meditation, a moment when you forget where you are or what time it is; you forget the body, the mind and the senses – all you are aware of is the Self – not the body which is your vehicle. You can see beyond the façade of the physical and you see the real Self within you, without face, without color or identity, without any kind of attributes - and that is your Source!

Unfortunately you don't always realize that. You are so identified and involved with the external, outer aspects of body, mind and senses, with your entire surroundings, that you consider this the Self. When you look into the mirror you say 'this is me' and that is when the trouble starts. You identified with your physical form.

Meditation should bring about a state of mind where you become one with yourself, when you realize that I AM not this, not that, not body, not mind, not the person associated with a given name. You realize that "I am beyond all that, the source of all happiness and bliss". During that state of meditation you have to ignore all your disturbing thoughts. When you concentrate on your breath, mind activity is somehow tamed and under control. The sounds of nature can assist you with this development. As I mentioned before, meditation is a gradual process wherein you move to the higher state of consciousness and where all the worldly problems that appear so huge, will become minute. That in itself is a wonderful transformation and achievement. All the things that have been bothering you so much will just become quite unimportant and irrelevant. Of course you feel relieved.

The process of meditation is a series of gradual steps, moving from body consciousness to mind, to soul, and finally to consciousness of Self. You begin to realize that all the many outer façades are just illusions, bubbles that were created and just dissolve again; they simply pop. All conflicts of life are temporary bubbles that come and go – they have to be accepted for what they are. They just appear and they vanish and you do not have to be distressed about this. Accepting these bubbles is part of life. Regard them as what they are: illusions and lessons to learn from.

Mind can and does create endless drama; it loves drama. That is the nature of mind. All you have to do is just wait, do the right thing and not get caught in the process. It will disappear. If you allow yourself to be caught you will multiply the drama and become its victim time and again. But when you make yourself the observer, you will be in control and master of each situation.

SOME THOUGHTS ON SELF DISCOVERY

In recent times health has become a major concern world wide – billions are spent on "getting healthy" through a variety of advertised diets, potions and supplements as well as gadgets for exercise. Despite all that, people are not healthy. This is a vital global issue.

Then the question arises why? If you look at the daily programming in the media, you may find some answers. Is it fair to say that 95% of news and entertainment is negative? Killings of men and beasts in countless varieties, rape, murder, stalking, torture, terror, incest, spousal, child and animal abuse dominate the "entertainment" that is offered. Is this what humans are supposed to feed on emotionally?

The more you explore and discover in the modern world the more arises a need for spiritual practices. This requires management of all kinds – especially important are physical health management and emotional management.

Can you maintain your physical body to be reasonably healthy and fit? For unless you are strong, fit and healthy with a mind that is unencumbered by some illness or discomfort you cannot proceed further. Therefore the first concern for each individual is health.

Of course, other discourses have referred to the basics – that is a healthy, balanced diet free of added chemicals as well as the need for regular exercise. Remember that the body is a magnificent piece of machinery; it needs fuel and it needs to move. There is a saying: "If you rest, you rust". Just simple stretching will benefit your body and its immune system. When you stretch you will feel your muscles activate your circulation – circulation will build your immune system. The better your immune system, the better are your chances of being fit and free from disease. Stretching is very important. Observe the children, stretching, running, laughing and crying, it is their natural ability and therapy. Unfortunately, when you grow, you lose such natural behavior.

The second concern is emotional management. How do you handle your anger, love, attachment, affection, and how do you react, interact, manage, receive and give? Do you laugh, do you cry? You should laugh and cry; there is nothing wrong with crying - although this seems to be easier for women who generally have an emotional make-up different from men. Crying can also be another form of anger, for when anger does not work, you may cry. At the same time anger should also not be suppressed, but rather released appropriately, not destructively.

Often, when anger is released, this can create hatred, which in turn can give rise to further anger and so on. The eventual result will be destruction. When you look at the wars, the terror and suffering today, you can see that all the conflicts are the result of anger and hatred, causing destruction and endless suffering.

The present time is one of the darkest times in the world, full of strife, war, terror and conflict. The greatest and most destructive element is religious hatred. Collectively this hatred is probably the worst hatred imaginable. History bears witness to this. Religious hatred is a great force, yet it is certainly not God who has created the problem; it is the followers or disciples identifying with only one or other limited understanding of the Almighty.

Just look and listen for a moment to what is going on around you today; it seems that every one is angry whether the subject of debate is race, country, ideology, religion or individuals. When you are angry, you want to destroy. Frequently the focus is very personal and centers on money or sex and rivalry. Anyone who is in disagreement with you, you may perceive as enemy. Then you focus your thoughts on how to overcome your enemy, if necessary on how to destroy him or her. But what you need to understand is that to really overcome your enemy you should pay them the least amount of attention, because that disempowers them. Become aware that your true and real enemies are your own negativities. You must learn how to handle those, lest they destroy you.

Love and hate have changed the world many times, both politically and economically. There are countless examples in history (*Anthony and Cleopatra)*. Both love and hate can create and change history - constructively as well as destructively. If you can recognize how to utilize these forces you can make them your friends. Such forces enable true power, but they must be used correctly. Anger management courses have increased exponentially with the emergence of worldwide anger. Learning to manage your own emotions can be the best service you can give yourself.

When you know how to handle your own emotions, you can help yourself and your loved ones, so that they become more capable of handling their emotions appropriately. People with health problems often live in emotional confusion; they do not know how to deal with their own emotions and they do not know how to deal with each other. The result is that they blame, complain, demand, and have expectations; the list is endless. The consequence is unhappiness.

Instead, try to learn how to be reasonable, see how much you can give, what you can tolerate and how and what you can receive. Giving endlessly is equally counterproductive. Food is good example. If you repeatedly eat too much of some delicious dish, instead of having an enjoyable experience, you will end up with indigestion, perhaps loss of sleep and eventual obesity. More is *not always* better; it will not make you happy. You have to learn to balance and manage quality and quantity.

Then how do you manage your emotions? First of all, do not hold a grudge against anyone; that way your mind is free. Emotions are a very complicated force and can truly enslave your mind. You should be able to interact with your loved ones and the not-so-loved ones without holding grudges, without suppressing wishes and desires, and without expectations.

People do not only have conflict with their fellow humans but also demand of their master, teacher or God that he or she should comply with whatever demands and wishes they might have - whatever package they might bring along - no matter how inappropriate the demands. They may ask for blessings, energy and fulfillment of their lower desires, not the higher aspirations. But how can God or Guru or teacher give if he can see that what you want is wrong for you? There is the problem; you base your demands and desires on your limited understanding and vision. Emotional management is very complex and difficult indeed – but that should not make you give up trying to bring balance into your lives.

The next aspect is Self-management. How well do you know yourself? You may know that you are more than body and mind, that you are much more than that; but how do you find out? Terms like nirvana and enlightenment have become well known words and you may believe that you are enlightened, but belief and faith can only take you so far. Ultimately it is the knowledge which triumphs, not the belief. Belief and faith have limitations. It is good to have belief and faith, for without that you cannot move, but belief and faith cannot take you to the ultimate fulfillment. For that you need knowledge and wisdom. I am not talking about knowledge that you learn at school or at college

– that is information. True knowledge is something else, something that will give you complete understanding of who and what you are. True knowledge resembles a blazing fire that will burn away all ignorance. Faith and trust, however, provide a far more gentle and easy aspect of growth.

Therefore, knowledge and wisdom are higher than faith and belief. Yet you need faith, love and trust in your teacher in order to receive the higher knowledge that is being transmitted. Insolence, rudeness, demands and lack of humility will get you nowhere. When you have the knowledge, then everything will make sense to you and all confusion will go. Again, emotion is concerned with faith and belief. You can communicate with your teacher or Guru or God through faith and love. When you establish this communication then you can receive and interact with him/her and you will have a two-way dialogue.

Communication of love, devotion and faith bind together – each emotion, each mental manifestation has powerful energy which helps you to move toward wholeness. People in the world as a whole can be happy, but for some reason this has not happened. If enough people understood that you can be happy, things would move in a different direction. Maybe God does not make it easy to really understand him/her; life resembles a play (*lila*) that continues on and on. You have the choice to get caught, or to observe, to participate or to be an onlooker, or to create and become master of this play. Essentially it is up to you which part you want to audition for in the cosmic play – select your role and you will earn your fruit accordingly.

All that we have talked about is part of self discovery; try to discover your happiness, and when you encounter any possible conflict, just regard it as a cloud – which will pass and the sun will come again – do not get caught in the cloud just let it pass and, let the sunshine come into your life.

- 33 -

PRACTICING ATTUNEMENT

Prayer: "I tune to you oh Lord, who will remove all negativity and install positivity and bliss."

When facing difficulties there is a tendency in people to look for an easy way out - easy things become popular and one does not really want to consider anything that involves hard work. Just think of the multiple shortcuts and labor-saving devices of modern daily life, from drive-ins to prepared food, instant coffee and instant anything; everything is prepared for you, and it is so convenient. When we perceive something as difficult and laborious, we actually make it so; the same applies if you consider something as easy.

If you develop spiritual understanding, things will just flow. Meaning and essence can be captured. For that you have to attune and 'connect'. When you have the connection it is not you who is speaking, rather the words come through you. You have to remove any fear and finally you are able to tune to your teacher who will speak through you. This is not hard work, you just have to tune into the right wavelength. Once that is achieved, you no longer have a problem. You do not need to plan or to prepare.

Whatever you focus on, whatever you tune into, you become *that.* Give this principle some thought. That is the law of psyche, of paranormal phenomena, that you become one with the object of your focus. That can be anything that your are in close contact with, no matter whether plant, animal, food, High Being, anything at all. You merge with that.

When you want something very badly your mind is focused on your desire, day and night, even on the mundane level. This meditation attracts the energy and provides the right attunement.

Svami Vivekananda went to the US to attend the Parliament of Religions in Chicago in 1893. He represented Hinduism and he was given 10 minutes to speak. He talked for over an hour to an absolutely spellbound audience. He had tuned to his guru, Sri Ramakrishna. When you are tuned to such a Being, He can motivate, inspire, guide and teach you. There is a constant interaction – a Spiritual Dialogue.

The cause of all conflict is non-communication. We do not communicate; we complain, grumble - and then we attack. Sometimes communication without talk contains a special energy. That has to be recognized and established. It has to do with opening oneself. Spiritual communication is a dialogue, a constant interaction. You can talk without a mediator, once you know how to. Communication just flows, the wind blows, the trees dance, the birds sing. There are many different types of communication without talk. You can communicate with yourself. However, total relaxation is required; it cannot be achieved while disturbed or anxious.

Can you make others feel comfortable and relaxed? If someone comes to you with a problem and that person is nervous, the first thing you have to do is to assist in relaxing the person. That art of relaxation you have to learn. For when you are relaxed, you are in control, make fewer mistakes; your senses are alert and you can react and respond more effectively.

Do not get this state confused with lethargy, carelessness or laziness. When relaxed, you can communicate much better. It is a recommended skill to acquire. For example, in daily life, in the case of a complaint, make the person comfortable; you can offer tea, coffee, etc to make them feel at ease. Chat for a while and by the time this is all done, the energy of the complaint- and negative reaction - is reduced, if not gone.

Some people have the skill to make you feel embarrassed for your own bad behavior, then you begin to blame and berate yourself. It is better to charm people than to be angry. You catch more flies with honey, than with vinegar.

If people follow the spiritual life, all those qualities will develop spontaneously, without effort. Consider this a by-product of spiritual practice. You begin to build a naturally positive personality and others around you will also be affected.

- 34 -

FLEXIBILITY AND STRENGTH

The dictionary describes flexibility as: *capable of being bent, usually without breaking* and strength is defined as *mental power, firmness and courage.*

The first sign of a real yogi is flexibility of body and mind. This is very important; it is also unusual in the average person. Yet you can bring flexibility and strength into the entire body and mind.

Rigidity in either body or mind can make or break either or both. You are all familiar with the example of a tree in the storm. If it can bend, it will generally survive; if it is rigidly defying the storm, the chances are that it will break or be uprooted. Even in the construction of a bridge, gaps have to be left to allow for expansion in a heatwave so that it can withstand all kinds of weather.

You have to endeavor to keep your body flexible and strong so that it can tolerate extremes of climate and the many daily conditions it may be exposed to. The mind also has to be trained to be flexible so that you will be able to cope with any crisis and any kind of news. Flexibility of mind also allows you to become balanced as regards to criticism and praise. A true yogi will be able to maintain equilibrium under any and all circumstances.

It is important to maintain balance in relation to life's challenges such as losses and gains. When you can maintain that state of mind, in all varieties of crises and changes, then you have mastered some spiritual achievement. If you can be angered easily, however, you have a long way to go.

Strength, inner strength, indicates an absence of fear. You know who and what you are and you have full confidence in yourself. What are the opinions of others, but reflections of their own limited minds? Why should that upset you?

There is an example in the life of the Buddha. Traveling through the country with his favorite disciple Ananda he gave talks at many places and – human ignorance and jealousy being what they are – was challenged and insulted at times. The Buddha paid no attention to the insults, but Ananda got very upset at the ignorance of people. Did they not know and realize that they were talking to a physical and spiritual prince? How could they not recognize a true master or teacher? The Buddha gave Ananda the analogy of a dog not being able to recognize the qualities of an elephant, yet still barking at the elephant. He went on to advise Ananda to be like the elephant instead, without fear, without insecurity, having full confidence in his own strength. "Know your own atma - your self - full of strength, without fear or insecurity. Wake up and regain what you have lost and restore your inner strength and be like the elephant and not like a mouse."

You may not be aware of this, but atman is the most dearly treasured part of you and it is because of your own atma that you love others. You are experiencing your own atma. You love yourself, your own atma and you are looking all over for this love. You are longing to bring back what you have lost.

It is only human wanting to be loved and liked, and if this does not happen, to become angry and upset. Wherever you may be, at any given place, if there is someone who likes you, you are happy - the ego also taking a slice of the credit. But if someone indicates dislike toward you, you become upset. "Why does that person not like me?" However, if you make an effort to understand others, to be flexible to their beliefs and understanding, they will like you. That is the key of how to turn people into friends. It is a simple skill: being charming is another skill, even if you do not feel like it. You lose nothing by being accommodating and flexible.

Discovery of yourself is the most important aspect of your development and your evolution. You can only love others if you love yourself. This is not to be mistaken with selfish love. It is not at all the same. Only when you love your atma will you know what love is. If you have never experienced happiness you cannot give it to others. You can only give what you have. If you have nothing, what can you give?

Sometimes I am asked: Why do so many High Beings keep themselves isolated from people? It is to gain the fullness of creation's condition that they want to experience. When that has been achieved, when they have gone through all pain and suffering, fearlessness, love and bliss, only then can they return and help people. In that context they are both flexible and strong and I can say that "those who do not worry, whose desire is gone, who do not need anything - they are the kings of kings."

CAN WE HAVE OPEN DEBATES/DISCUSSIONS?

Question: Svamiji, you had mentioned before that people should have an open debate with God, and that we could discuss anything directly with God. How does that work? How is it possible to communicate and debate directly with God?

Svamiji: Well, this is really a 2-part question. Let us look at the basics of an open debate first.

Open debate seems to be one of the most difficult things in the world. On the individual level, family level, social, community, national and international level, how many truly open and non-rehearsed debates have you ever observed? Is it fair to assume that you have *never* witnessed such a debate? People like closed-door sessions based on the motto: "You scratch my back and I'll scratch yours", an arrangement that is advantageous to all those involved. An open door session is something that is very rare deed; it contains confrontation, and true confrontation can be very uncomfortable.

People do not want a confrontation or to have a dialogue or debate, because of fear. The fear of losing, of appearing unimportant, of being humiliated or rejected will outweigh all other reasons.

So, being fearful, who can debate? Who can have an open dialogue? Who can manage to be truthful? Only one who has no fear, no insecurities, one who follows the truth and who has nothing to lose and nothing to hide. If you consider all these qualities, how many people are left? I'm afraid not many.

On this basis open debate or dialogue seem to be out of the question. Even on an individual basis, like two friends talking person to person, you will encounter difficulties. The moment your friend starts to assert his/her point, you react and become defensive, and when you become defensive, you react and you lose objectivity. Not only do you continue to defend yourself, but you will go on the offensive. When defense does not work, offensive is the next step. In that state, you may scream, shout or abuse and if that is not enough, rage can set in and you can become violent. All these reactions are processes prompted by ego. This is not communication. It is not a dialogue – and not a debate. The best you can call it is an argument or a fight.

How can you have an open debate when the other party, other person, other group, when the other side's mind is already set and is not willing and ready for open debate? It is essential that all parties are willing to listen with an open mind to the others and then state their own points of view.

It is important to remember the thinking power that humans are blessed with. Right thinking and mindfulness are vital qualities for true participation in life's debate and discussions. Yet thinking is difficult whereas not thinking is very easy, just going with the flow... you get up, you brush your teeth, go through the motions of the day, breakfast, lunch, supper, work, play, interaction with others, maybe some gossip, and then you are tired and you go to sleep. Where in all this is real thought involved? No-where! You become like a robot. You are programmed to do these things. You have been following this routine since you were born. You do the same thing over and over again - it has become second nature. It does not take much effort, much thinking, and much consciousness, to continue doing what you have been used to. But then the day may come when you begin to question.

Questioning yourself is the difficult part. It triggers your psychology. It opens up the emotions and the path to a true dialogue. The way of open dialogue is a noble way that has been followed throughout the ages. Your experiences in the world today are mostly monologue. Your parents tell you what to do, so you do it. Your teacher tells you what to do, so you do it; in the workplace your boss tells you what to do, so you do it; and then your friends tell you what to do and you do that too — it's all monologue. Dialogue is very much missing. When you chat, what do you chat about? You have nothing much to talk about except who has what, who went with whom, who's having an affair with whom, who bought what, who went where, and normal gossip - that is what is mostly talked about. Meaningful conversations are rare.

Once I was with a small group and we met with a diplomat, a *chargé d'affaires* of a middle European country. We had expected an interesting discussion based on the publication of a book dealing with the former political climate. However it turned out that this gentleman was an expert on a variety of wine and he presented us with his knowledge of wine, in great detail – a subject we could not debate, since he was the expert. You have to agree with the experts, and he was the expert in wine drinking. That's all he knew. That's all he could offer and that was the end of the dialogue. I said "fine" and that concluded our meeting. All of us went home and had tea: he went home and had wine. So how can you have a dialogue? It is like dealing with two totally different concepts.

Having a dialogue with yourself is a very fascinating experience, because you have the guru, the teacher, sitting inside you. This is a practical aspect of the debate with God. You think you are alone. You are not all alone; you are several identities. You don't realize that you are several beings within your being. For instance, when you sleep very deeply, you say, "I slept very well." If you slept very well, who was watching? There had to be a second being who was watching that you slept very well. There had to be a different identity who observed how you slept.

Have you had a dialogue with your own guru within you? You can start a dialogue with your own self. Now, some people talk to themselves, which is different, more like a mind-chatter that goes on within the person; it is more like complaining, blaming and re-arranging a situation. This is not a real dialogue. Some people have a tendency to grumble, especially when they become older. It becomes second nature to keep on talking whether somebody hears or not; perhaps by talking that way they relieve their tension and anxiety.

But how do you start a true dialogue with yourself? How can you have a dialogue with God? Supposing you read the *Bhagavad Gita* and you think about and contemplate every word that Krishna says. When you have a question, you invite him and you ask him, "What do you mean by this?" He will reply.

In the books of many religions the question arises as to whether Jesus, Mohammed or anyone else actually said all that is written or whether somebody else decided to say it in his name? Before you can have a dialogue with God, you have to contemplate the teachings first. For instance, before you want to have a dialogue with me, you have to read my works first and not only read them, but also contemplate them. After you have read and contemplated, after you have reflected enough and when you have understood and implemented my teachings, then you can have a dialogue with me and then you will listen. How can you have a dialogue without listening and without understanding? You need to connect yourself through the higher level of interaction.

On some level of communication, it is like lying on the psychologist's sofa, relating your problems and concerns. That is not a dialogue or communication. It is a monologue although in a way it is a guided monologue. With the psychologist, you are relaxed on the sofa and you feel like you can tell everything; you feel that someone is listening and you can unburden yourself – and that itself can be therapeutic.

A real debate about higher values also represents a vital aspect of life, assisting the debate with God. For example, when I say that open debate is the answer to world peace, that is an idea, it is a noble thought. However, where this is going to take place in reality is a big question.

Frequently you see so-called open debates on television; they are far from being open debates – everything is controlled and rehearsed. Everything is prepared in advance, edited and controlled. It may appear as open debate, yet it is far from it. Before every interview I have ever had on television or radio, a reporter or presenter has had to discuss the details with me in advance. All of them have said, "I will ask you this and what will you reply?" And I say "I will reply that ." Interviewers want to make sure that I will not say anything publicly that can be offensive or outrageous, that could be damaging to their interests. I might speak out against the media, or I might say something for which they are not prepared. I have never been invited to go and speak my mind.

So that is your media. You cannot have an open debate, it is not possible. But if the time should come in the future and we can have an open debate, not only on TV but also at home, a lot of problems can be solved. The difficulty is that whenever you have open debates, you will create a lot of enemies and you do not really want to do that, because you already have more than you can cope with and you do not want to create more enemies.

Effectively it is not possible to tell the truth or speak your mind, but that does not mean that you cannot practice the truth. As I have said, the truth is your birthright, and you can individually follow and practice the truth. However please do not expect the world to be ready for your truth.

On a lower level of consciousness, you are not emotionally prepared to hold the truth, and so you compromise. You compromise for the sake of coexistence. As long as you compromise for the greater good, it seems to be productive. If, however, you compromise your fundamental self, then you are actually losing, because you are sacrificing yourself and your happiness in vain for someone else's vanity, greed or satisfaction. You have to learn to strike a balance. A stanza in the Vedas reminds us: "Speak the Truth, but do not speak bitter Truth". You can state your expressions and opinions firmly, but without insult and malice or the intent to hurt the other party. Bitter truth is very hurtful. Truth spoken kindly may bring a positive response. I can recommend this method.

I have always been ready for debate throughout time and when people realize that I am ready for debate, they generally back down, because they are not ready and they feel they will lose, because they are insecure and fearful. Yet I am trying to make people aware, to bring them truth and knowledge, to make them strong and powerful, so they will be so strong and so powerful that no one can trick them. True knowledge is the most powerful tool you have. When you have knowledge, no one can defeat you.

Just imagine that somebody lives 60 or 70 years and he/she lived a life of lies. Later, maybe during a debate or dialogue, that person realizes that he/she had practiced and believed in something that was false and untrue. What a devastating effect! Although one can accept the truth at any stage of life, truth is truth. That is where the debate would stop, because the fear of losing what you have built for years may be just too overwhelming. If you have built a life on lies, being faced with the truth can shatter your life like glass.

The Italian Galileo was persecuted by the church and he had to suppress the truth [that the earth revolved around the sun] – a problem for the orderly, comprehensive picture of the *geocentric model* of the universe at that time, in which everything circled around the Earth. When he was dying, he renounced the lie he had been forced to proclaim, and that what he was stating now was the TRUTH. He realized that he was dying and he had nothing to lose; he could afford to speak the truth at the time of his death.

When considering a debate with God it is also helpful to understand and recall that the play of the Maya, the great illusion, is always part of Life and we all have parts in the big play. The world is a stage and we are all little and big players. The question is who plays fairly and who plays unfairly? Life can be a lot of fun, full of happiness and laughter, but, of course, you cannot avoid some tragedy. The point is that you do not have to invite drama; it is all around you in any case. But to create counter-drama is something you have to make an effort to do. Drama is everywhere. It is up to you to create the right environment for your own peace of mind and your own happiness. Mindfulness and positive attitude enable more enlightened debate.

As I said, open debate in the normal world is always subjective, because very few people can accept the truth, even fewer practice it. Yet history is full of people who, against all odds, have practiced the truth. Mahatma Gandhi called his life "an experiment with truth". There was a time in Ancient India when the truth of Divine Teaching had become obscured and confused with the arrival of Buddhism. Gautam, the Buddha had been raised in the Hindu religion, yet having observed the many aberrations of religion at that time, he tried to bring truth back into the lives of the people. Since humans like to create new things, the followers of Buddha, the Enlightened One, named it Buddhism and considered themselves separate from the Hindus, resulting in further confusion.

Not until the arrival of the young Shankaracharya (believed to be an incarnation of Siva) did things change. The 13-year old decided to set things straight. By traversing the country on foot he invited debates with the learned ones of that time. The approach was that the one who lost the debate became the disciple of the winner. Everyone was in agreement. At least at that time people were ready to debate. For many years he continued to walk the vast country, debating. People came to listen and enjoyed the debates. They also learned from the debates. Within these debates lies the origin of true democracy. Through such debates more enlightened dialogue and discussions were possible.

Western society claims to practice democracy and debate. In principle this is correct, in practice not. You cannot get away with speaking your mind publicly in politics. Party politics will not let you. You would be black-listed or expelled and again: People are afraid to become negatively targeted. The time of Shankaracharya thus was the first and last time in history that open debate took place. This kind of debate may be a model, an ideal, but no-one can prevent you from having a debate with yourself. Then you can invite God, present your question, and providing you are clear in your mind what you are asking, you *will* get an answer.

TALKS AND QUESTIONS WITH SRI SVAMIJI

Question: Svamiji, could you please explain to us the importance of *Pranayama*–breath control-and give us some instructions for practice?

Svamiji: As most of you know, *Pranayama* is the control, regulation, and integration of *prana*, the energy source by which life is sustained. It is sometimes referred to as the 'breath of life'. *Pranayama* is a *Sanskrit* term composed of two words, *prâna*, life force, or vital energy, and *yâma*, control. Therefore *Pranayama* becomes the energy source by which life is sustained. It is your own energy and that of your environment. As you inhale, you take in air and life energy. Exhaling, you expel the waste products of your body's metabolism.

Most people go about their lives quite unaware of the importance of effective breathing. Often the breathing is shallow and rapid, providing insufficient ventilation of the lungs which can and does eventually result in disease.

Before considering any kind of special breathing exercises, it is necessary to correct any existing faulty techniques and truly learn to *breathe.* The air we breathe is designed to enter the human body via the nose. This organ is equipped with fine hairs to filter dirt and dust; it has the ability to moisten and warm the air; and of course it has the sense of smell which warns us of unhealthy, poisonous, or toxic substances. To breathe effectively, inhale through the nose, keep an upright posture, avoid highly polluted surroundings such as smoky rooms, and whenever you can during the day, spend a few minutes breathing deeply, fully, and slowly, without straining. Implementation of these few simple instructions alone can bring you renewed energy and well-being as well as a strengthened immune system.

As part of a healthy routine it is recommended to practise *pranayama* for 30 minutes daily-or at least 10–15 minutes-to benefit body, mind, thoughts and emotions.

It is a good idea to have your lung quality checked by your medical adviser. It is a simple and fairly accurate test of a few minutes – if the test indicates that your lung/breath capacity is low, this can be a sign of poor physical and mental health. This is the time to do *pranayama.*

Breathing patterns should be affecting all seven energy centers or chakras of the human body. Whereas most people breathe superficially, when you do *pranayama* you learn to breathe deeply affecting all organs and chakras.

Question: How far can we benefit from meditation when practicsing *pranayama*?

Svamiji: I would suggest the following form of *pranayama* meditation.

Breathe slowly in and out, concentrate on the breath and relax the entire system – the body, the mind and also the senses.

Feel light all around you, then light and energy inside you. Your body is your lighthouse, your mind is filled with light energy - your senses are filled with light – every part of your body is being charged with light energy – all impurities are leaving you, you are becoming purified, free from disease and free from pain and suffering. Your entire being is filled with light-energy.

Do not try to control your mind, rather let mind wander and follow it instead. As you follow your mind you will find that mind is no longer interested in details but rather in substance.

Let mind feel and visualize all aspects within and without. You become the observer, witness, onlooker and do not get involved – just watch – your body, watch your senses, watch your feelings, emotions, watch your duality - both the negative and the positive, bad and good, low and high - watch them all without getting involved. You are not your mind, you are not your senses, and you are not your physical aspects.

You are in control and you are in command – you are the Ultimate, the Whole and you are the Complete. These are all your manifestations – observe them and watch the play, the *lila.*

Watch and observe, feel and enjoy the beautiful aspects of the cosmos and nature's manifestation without and within, repeating the sacred sound Om –SoHam.

Question: How do we attune to the Cosmic Energy with this practice and meditation?

Svamiji: Through such ongoing practice we invoke the energy, the Great Power and the Great Source and we tune to the breath and the cosmic power which is right within and around us, meaning "I Am That I Am" - I am the beginning, the middle and the end. I am beyond time - Akala – beyond space, the Source, the Whole, the Complete, everything that is manifest. The interpretations can be endless to seek meaning and to activate and enforce this attunement.

In the world humans have forgotten their true identity and identify with the physical body alone. Many have gone to the lowest of low and that is why there is a feeling of helplessness and of desperate unhappiness. Humans need to be uplifted from a feeling of inadequacy to return to their original Self and to find their true Self.

It is necessary to return to that state of conscious fulfillment, where every moment of your life is filled with happiness, where you can enjoy nature like the song of the birds, the wind in the trees, the glow of a mountain sunset, the lapping of ocean waves. You have the power to remind yourself who and what you really are, through thought, reflection, analysis and through contemplation and meditation.

The journey of life never ends – there is no beginning and no end. The circle of life is infinite – how many lives will it take to complete the circle? Each time you join the great spiritual debate and practice you are meant to resolve the mystery – or at least part of the mystery. There are countless mysteries and the intention is to unravel them – one by one. The spiritual journey is not for entertainment, although, at times, it can be very entertaining. Essentially the discovery of your Self is a serious matter.

Question: How important is this search?

Svamiji: Through this search one achieves true happiness and fearlessness. In modern life all kinds of discoveries come onto the daily market; each one becomes a big sensation, yet the discovery of your personal journey is much more exciting and fulfilling. It cannot compare to anything else. It is an ongoing process, not just a limited time course, but a continuing experience of unfoldment and discovery. It is the key of your life - and many lives. Really, there is no way out – you have to do it, you have to go through it. The whole idea of having a human life is to discover the ultimate Truth. If you fail, you may have to evolve through many more lives to become human again. There is no need to wait for happiness at the end of the road, be happy now! All the ingredients for happiness are right here.

Kabir, the ancient mystic and poet, stated it beautifully: "Oh Man, why are you looking all around you, when I am right here with you, look at me, find me, I am the puzzle and the mystery. Solve the riddle and find me; I am just here with you."

Only those who speak the truth, who have no fear, are enlightened. Only when you feel you have nothing to lose, and nothing to gain, can you be fearless. However, when you feel that there is still a lot to lose, you will live in fear. As long as you feel that you have anything to lose you cannot be fearless. Once you have become fearless, you are on the Path of enlightenment.

GLOSSARY OF SANSKRIT TERMS

Atma(n)	The Self, the Immortal Soul.
Ashram	Training school for spiritual aspirants.
Bhagavad Gita	"The Divine Song" - a celebrated mystical poem of 18 chapters, containing the sacred dialogue between *Krisna* and *Arjuna*. A major spiritual and philosophical treatise; the source book of Hindu philosophy.
Buddha	**Siddhartha Gautama**, Divine Incarnation – teacher of Spiritual Truths and historical founder of Buddhism.
Gayatri	Gayatra - a hymn, a song composed in the gayatri meter, consisting of 24 syllables, generally as a triplet of 8 syllables each; the sacred verse of praise to the Creator. *Om Bhur Bhuvah Svah* *Tat Savitur Varenyam* *Bhargo Devasya Dhimahi* *Dhiyo Yo Nah Prachodayat*
Guru	*Gu* – darkness; *ru* – light; the preceptor or spiritual guide who takes you from the darkness of spiritual doubt into the light of true knowledge.

Hatha Yoga	Ha – sun; tha – moon: physical exercises which promote the balancing of positive and negative energies within the body (see: yoga).
Kabir	14th century mystic poet of India revered by Hindus, Sikhs and Moslems alike. Kabir, in his simple, straightforward approach (2-line dohas) gave a new direction to Indian philosophy. *Example:* "Like the seed contains the oil and the fire is in the flint stone, thus in your temple seats the Divine. Realize this if you can."
Karma	Action, work, deeds, performance, the result of one's actions.
Karma Yoga	The yoga of selfless action – not seeking recognition or reward for one's actions.
Krisna (Krishna)	Divine Incarnation of Vishnu–Stories and teachings associated with him represent an integral part of Hindu philosophy with applications for daily living.
Mantra(m)	Concentrated energy of certain sacred sound syllables (see the discourse: Mantras).
Marpa	See **Milarepa** below.
Maya	The great illusion of the world as reality; Mother Nature.
Milarepa	**Jetsun Milarepa** was one of Tibet's most famous yogis and poets. He began his

	career by studying sorcery. Realizing the horrendous karmic repercussions of such focus, he surrendered to the Master **Marpa**, the Translator. Only through complete trust, dedication and diligence was he able to overcome the very harsh lessons and tasks his Guru assigned to him. Eventually Milarepa achieved highest state of enlightenment.
Purna	Whole: is derived from root "Pri" meaning to fill. Thus Purna means full or complete. Purna can also be interpreted to mean infinity, totality and completeness.
Sage	Wise or holy person, philosopher (see Milarepa).
Seva	Selfless service without expectation of recognition or reward.
Spiritual Teacher	See "guru".
Tulsidas	**Goswami Tulsidas** (*1532-1623*) Indian *poet* and *philosopher* saint - considered one of the greatest and most famous of Indian poets. He is regarded as an incarnation of *Valmiki*, author of the epic *Ramayana* written in *Sanskrit*.
Vedas	Literally: true knowledge; ancient, sacred texts of civilization, consisting of four collections: *Rigveda* – dealing with true knowledge; *Samveda*–science of sound; *Yayurveda* – dealing with aspects of health and medicine; *Atharvaveda* – dealing with the aspects of Nature

Vedanta — System of knowledge based on the essence of the Vedas, concerning the nature and relationships of three principles:

1. *The Ultimate Principle;*
2. *The world; and*
3. *The individual soul.*

Yayurveda — See Vedas.

Viveka — Discrimination on the basis of foregone investigation, resulting in true knowledge.

Yoga — Literally: union; derived from the root YUK, meaning to join, also translates as "yoke" Impulses and inclinations of the ever wavering mind are brought under the discriminating yoke of the Higher Self. There are different types of yoga, each starting with a different aspect – all leading towards harmony and integration of the whole being.

BOOKS OF RELATED INTEREST FROM NAB

FINDING SOUL IN WORK AND LIFE
—*Prafulla Raval & Vasant Raval*
Spirituality transcends religion, rituals, dogmas and rules. The authors here try to explain in a systematic manner the meaning and role of spirituality in lives and how to get it, trickle by trickle, until the bucket is full.

ISBN: 978-81-7822-353-7

HOW TO DEVELOP YOUR PSYCHIC POWERS: Art and Science of Psychic Healing—Larry M. McDaniel & *Phyllis G. McDaniel*
The book explores understanding of Auras and brings about an awareness of the spiritual self. The concerns of modern era, finances, romance and focus on the future are given a psychic interpretation, placing the self as supreme.

ISBN: 978-81-7822-326-1

ROADSIGNS ON THE SPIRITUAL PATH: Living at Heart of Paradox—*Philip Goldberg*
This is one of the wisest books to appear in recent years about the perils and promises that are routinely encountered by all spiritual seekers. At a time in history when people are desperately grasping for security and certainty, Roadsigns is an invaluable contribution from a very wise spiritual teacher.

ISBN: 978-81-7822-342-1

YOGA IN MODERN INDIA: The Body between Science and Philosophy—*Joseph S. Alter*
Based on extensive ethnographic research and an analysis of both ancient and modern texts, *Yoga in Modern India* examines the history of yoga, focusing on its emergence in modern India and its dramatically changing form and significance in the twentieth century. Much of the book is quite accessible to the general reader, and many of Alter's more theoretical and analytical interpretations of modern understandings of yoga, health, medicine, the body, and truth claims are novel and stimulating.

ISBN: 978-81-7822-324-7

THE NOTEBOOKS OF PAUL BRUNTON IN 16 VOLS.

Perspectives (Vol-1): An inspiring insight into the essence of East-West spiritual philosophy.

The Quest (Vol-2): The Quest gives timely, candid, immediately useful advice about the promises and pitfalls of spiritual seeking.

Practices for The Quest Relax and Retreat (Vol-3): The book goes directly to the heart of exercises, techniques, and mental attitudes useful for spiritual self-discovery and self-development.

Meditation (Vol-4, Part-1): Meditation is an inspiring invitation to the most adventure of human spirituality—the direct experience of one's own beloved soul.

The Body (Vol-4, Part-2): The body is a balanced course in perceiving and perfecting the physical body's potential to become an eloquent expression of the divine force within.

Emotions of Ethics: The Intellect (Vol-5): The book is a detailed guide to its spiritual development.

The Ego: From Birth to Rebirth (Vol-6): The ego is a unique and unprecedented contribution to the literature of self-realization.

Healing of the Self: The Negatives (Vol-7): The book treats the mind – body relationship and contrasts conventional, psychic and spiritual approaches to healing.

Reflections on My Life and Writings (Vol-8): The book contains Paul Brunton's reflections about himself through fifty years of research, practice and writing.

Human Experience: The Arts in Culture (Vol-9): It teaches us to convert our lives into a process of spiritual discoveries and explores causes and purposes of suffering, problems of marriage and other relationships.

The Orient: Its Legacy to the West (Vol-10): Providing a fascinating view of traditional and contemporary oriental life, the book highlights the colours from Himalayan countries.

The Sensitives: Dynamics and Dangers of Mysticism (Vol-11): The Sensitives is a timely, informed evaluation of mysticism, "paranormal" experience, sects and cults.

The Religious Urge (Reverential Life) (Vol-12): The book distinguishes the heart's ineradicable religious instinct from traditional religious forms.

Relativity, Philosophy and Mind (Vol-13): The author explains the philosophy of the science of the deeper levels of mind. There is a deep meaning associated with our sleep and dreams.

Inspiration and The Overself (Vol-14): The book explains the tests and methods to develop intuitions, making it a vitalizing power for our existence.

Advanced Contemplation: The Peace Within You (Vol-15): The author believes that there is indeed no short path to peace within oneself and the book is an uplifting approach to the peace within.

Enlightened Mind, Divine Mind (Vol-16)—The book discovers a strong, controversial and definitive account of what "Enlightenment" is. The book outlines the stages in spiritual hierarchy of mystics, saints, messengers, prophets, sages and avatars.